Soupmeals

Soups to feed body, soul & friends

Hardie Grant

PUBLISHING

Soupmeals

EMILY EZEKIEL

PHOTOGRAPHY BY ISSY CROKER

contents
..

Introduction

..

Soup Meals is a recipe book inspired by the changing of the seasons. Using the best seasonal produce, you can easily make delicious and all around satisfying meals, which are healthy and full of flavor.

This book will show you how to use each season's produce to mix things up—so get rid of those boring, flavorless store-bought soups and bring in punchy flavors, textures, and easy add-ins.

Here, you really will eat the rainbow of vegetables throughout the whole year, not only making your food shop more sustainable but better for your overall health. Soups are pure joy in a bowl, and with so much fresh produce available, your options are endless.

..

Soup essentials
..

Pantry staples

When it comes to what to I keep in my pantry, it's always the same: jars of good-quality jars beans, as they add protein and bulk out most dishes; bottles of olive oil; and high-quality spices such as za'atar, sweet smoked paprika, and hot pepper flakes.

1.Spices
Keep coriander, cumin, sweet smoked paprika, hot pepper flakes, and gochujang (Korean pepper flakes) in stock.

2. Maple syrup
This is very useful for adding sweetness to soups.

3. Noodles
Store a selection of noodles, such as rice, egg, and Vietnamese banh pho noodles for Asian-style soups.

4. Crispy onions
These are great to add as a garnish to soups (see page 178 for the recipe).

5. Breads
Breads, such as sourdough, make good accompaniments to soup and also for making croutons and crumbs.

6. Oils & vinegars
Store good-quality olive oil and red and white wine vinegars to add flavor and depth to soups.

Tools

Everyone needs their favorite equipment to keep them cooking. If you invest in a sharp knife and a good-quality vegetable peeler you will be set. When it comes to soups it's really worth investing in a stick blender. As you become more confident in the kitchen and work your way through the following recipes, invest in the equipment that will make your life that bit easier.

1. Heavy saucepan
A large, heavy saucepan or stockpot is a must-have for making soup.

2. Sharp knife
Invest in a good-quality sharp knife to help you prepare food quickly and safely.

3. Stick blender
This blender makes it much easier to blend cooked ingredients into soup.

4. Cutting board
A must-have in the kitchen when chopping or slicing vegetables and herbs.

5. Ladle
Ladles, whether wooden or metal, are ideal for serving soup into bowls.

6. Microplane
A must-have tool for zesting citrus fruits.

artichokes

As artichokes have a delicate, sweet flavor, they make great soups. Use artichoke hearts.

radishes

There are a variety of ways that you can use spring radishes in soups, including lightly roasting them and quick pickling.

onions

Red, yellow, or white onions are perfect for making into soup. Try the recipe on page 27.

leeks

Leeks have a mild, sweet flavor, which pairs well with potatoes, especially in the Leek & Potato Soup on page 135.

celery

Celery has a strong but mild flavor and pairs well with other vegetables, including spring greens.

spinach

As spinach is packed with nutrients, it is a great addition to soups. Try the recipe on page 25.

peppers

Peppers have a sweet and mild flavor and partner well with herbs and spices, such as sweet smoked paprika and fresh parsley.

fava beans

Young fava beans have a delicate flavor so go well with spring greens. If you have a glut of them, try adding them to soup.

asparagus

You can use both the spears and stems in soup, which helps to reduce food waste.

cucumber

Cucumbers are hydrating so make a refreshing soup in the spring. Try the recipe on page 19.

carrots

Spring carrots are tender and very sweet, so are perfect for making into a soup, such as the one on page 27.

spring greens

Spring greens are the earliest variety of cabbage in the year and add a fresh flavor to soups in this season.

parsley

Fresh parsley has an herbal taste so adding it to soups gives them a greater depth of flavor.

kale

You can use both the stems and leaves in chunky-style soups, such as the Minestrone on page 45.

Spring

new potatoes

New potatoes keep their shape once they are cooked, so they are perfect for chunky soups, such as the one on page 25.

cauliflower

Cauliflower has a mild and nutty taste with bitter undertones, and partners well with Indian spices. Try the recipe on page 17.

scallions

Scallions are sweeter and milder than regular onions. Try the Scallion Congee on page 35.

watercress

Watercress has a slightly bitter, peppery flavor and goes well with many vegetables, such as carrots and beets.

beets

Beets are best from spring until early winter. They have a sweet, earthy taste that goes well with warming spices and Greek yogurt.

Brussels sprouts

Brussels sprouts are available right through until March. They have a nutty flavor and are great paired with lime.

Spring has sprung with this deliciously light and tasty soup. As this soup is so versatile, use any greens that are in season.

Spring greens soup

with grated pecorino

PREP TIME: 10 minutes   COOK TIME: 25 minutes   SERVES: 2

3 shallots

4 garlic cloves

2 celery stalks

2 handfuls of spring greens

8 asparagus stalks

scant ½ cup (100ml) olive oil

1 large glass of white wine

juice of ½ lemon

3¼ cups (800ml) chicken stock

1 large pinch of hot pepper flakes

1 handful of podded fava beans

2 handfuls of Sourdough
  Croutons (page 179)

salt and ground black pepper

grated pecorino cheese,
  for serving

Finely slice the shallots and garlic, then dice the celery. Thinly slice the spring greens and chop the asparagus. Set aside.

Heat the olive oil in a medium, heavy saucepan over medium heat. Add the shallots, celery, and garlic and fry for 10 minutes, stirring often.

Pour in the wine and lemon juice and sprinkle in the hot pepper flakes. Simmer for 5 minutes, then add the stock. Bring back to a rolling boil and add the fava beans, asparagus, and spring greens. Simmer for 10 minutes, then taste and adjust the seasoning to your liking.

Ladle into two bowls, top with croutons and a flurry of grated pecorino, and serve.

STORE/MAKE IT VEGAN
For a vegan option, simply use vegetable stock and omit the cheese.

Watercress & Stilton soup

with a rye-baked crouton crumb

PREP TIME: 10 minutes   COOK TIME: 30 minutes   SERVES: 2

• •

2 tablespoons butter

2 tablespoons olive oil

2 leeks, finely sliced

2 celery stalks, thinly sliced

1 large glass of white wine

1 potato, peeled and cubed

3¼ cups (800ml) chicken or
   vegetable stock

5¾ ounces (160g) watercress

⅔ cup (150ml) crème fraîche

3 ounces (80g) Stilton

1 large handful of Rye-Baked
   Crouton Crumb (page 179)

a drizzle of Parsley Oil (page 200)

salt and ground black pepper

Heat a large saucepan over medium heat, then add the butter and olive oil. Add the sliced leeks and celery, reduce the heat to low, and fry for 10 minutes, or until the leeks are soft and sticky. Pour in the wine and turn the heat up for a minute.

Add the cubed potato and stock, bring to a boil, then reduce the heat and simmer for 15 minutes, or until the potato is cooked.

Drop in the watercress and simmer for another 3 minutes. Remove the pan from the heat and add the crème fraîche and half the Stilton. Blend with a handheld blender until smooth. Season to taste with salt and pepper.

Ladle into bowls, top with the crouton crumb and remaining cheese, then drizzle with a little parsley oil. Serve.

• •

STORE/MAKE IT VEGAN

For a vegan option, use vegan versions of butter and crème fraîche, omit the cheese, and add 1 tablespoon miso and 2 tablespoons nutritional yeast when blending.

This creamy, well-spiced cauliflower soup is often what I think of when I see cauliflowers in a market. The soup freezes really well.

Spiced Indian cauliflower soup

with crispy naan toppers

PREP TIME: 10 minutes   COOK TIME: 30 minutes   SERVES: 2

• •

12 ounces (350g) cauliflower,
    outer leaves removed
¼ cup (60g) ghee
2 onions, thinly sliced
5 garlic cloves, grated
2½-inch (6cm) piece
    gingerroot, grated
1 teaspoon ground turmeric

2 tablespoons tikka paste
juice of 1 lemon
generous 2 cups (500ml)
    chicken stock
1 naan bread
2 tablespoons Indian Curry Leaf
    & Seed Oil (page 201)
salt

Cut the cauliflower into small florets and set aside. Heat 3 tablespoons of the ghee in a large wide-bottomed saucepan. Add the onions and fry for 10 to 15 minutes. Add the garlic and gingerroot and fry for another 5 minutes.

Add the cauliflower, turmeric, and tikka paste to the pan and fry for 2 minutes, stirring all the time. Add the lemon juice and stock and simmer for 15 minutes, or until the cauliflower is soft.

Meanwhile, preheat the oven to 400°F (200°C).

Slice the naan into 1¼-inch- (3cm)-long pieces and arrange the slices on a large baking sheet. Drizzle with the remaining ghee, season with salt, and bake in the oven for 10 minutes, or until crisp and golden, turning halfway through.

When the soup is ready, blend with a stick blender until smooth. Taste and adjust the seasoning. Ladle into bowls, drizzle over the seed oil, and serve with the naan.

• •

STORE/MAKE IT VEGAN
To make this soup vegan, use neutral oil instead of ghee, swap the chicken stock for vegetable, and make sure the naan is vegan.

This soup is very refreshing and delicious in those warmer spring days. You can chill this soup and serve it whenever you fancy it.

Cold cucumber soup

with crunchy toppings

PREP TIME: 5 minutes   COOK TIME: 0 minutes   SERVES: 2

6 Persian cucumbers, thinly sliced
scant 1 cup (200g) Greek yogurt
1 handful of basil
¼ cup (60ml) olive oil
juice of ½ lemon
¾ cup (100g) blanched
    almonds, toasted
2 tablespoons fresh dill

2 jalapeño chiles, sliced
1 dill pickle, sliced
1 handful of Rye-Baked Crouton
    Crumb (page 179)

Add the cucumber, yogurt, basil, most of the oil, keeping a little aside for the top, all the lemon juice, half the almonds, and a small amount of the dill to a high-speed blender and blend until smooth.

Pour into bowls and top with the remaining almonds, dill, sliced chiles, dill pickle, and crouton crumb. Drizzle with the remaining oil and serve.

STORE/MAKE IT VEGAN
For a vegan option, use coconut yogurt instead of Greek yogurt.

This is my take on a classic Vietnamese street food dish Pho. Use wide rice noodles if you can't find banh pho.

Lemongrass chicken pho

with fresh herbs, bean sprouts & chile

PREP TIME: 5 minutes   COOK TIME: 35 minutes   SERVES: 2

• •

1 head of spring greens
1 lemongrass stalk, finely sliced
1 tablespoon peanut oil
4 chicken thighs, skin on and
   bone in, 5 ounces (140g) each
2½ cups (600ml) Spiced Broth
   (page 177)
3½ ounces (100g) banh pho noodles

1 tablespoon fish sauce
1 bunch of Thai basil
1 handful of mint
1 small bunch of cilantro
1 handful of bean sprouts
1 red chile, sliced
1 lime, cut into wedges
salt

Finely slice the spring greens and set aside, then finely slice the lemongrass and set aside. Heat the oil in a large, wide saucepan over medium heat. Season the chicken thighs with salt and fry, skin-side down, for 10 minutes. Turn the chicken over and toss in the lemongrass. Pour in the broth, reduce the heat, and simmer for 20 minutes.

Meanwhile, cook the noodles according to the package directions, then drain and rinse under cold water. Set aside.

Once the chicken is cooked, remove from the pan and slice the meat off the bone.

Add the spring greens and fish sauce to the broth and cook for 5 minutes. Return the chicken meat to the pan.

Divide the noodles between bowls and pour over the soup. Serve with a side plate of the herbs, bean sprouts, chile, and lime wedges.

• •

STORE/MAKE IT VEGAN
Store any leftover soup in an airtight container in the refrigerator for up to three days. It's best to remove the noodles and store them separately.

• •

This decadent French onion soup is a go-to when new-season onions are available as they are so sweet and delicious.

French onion soup

with sourdough cheese toasts

PREP TIME: 15 minutes   COOK TIME: 1 hour   SERVES: 2

• •

¾ stick (75g) unsalted butter

3 large white onions, sliced into
  half-moons

2 red onions, sliced into
  half-moons

2 tablespoons all-purpose flour

1 small bunch of thyme leaves

10 sage leaves

1¼ cups (300ml) dry white wine

3¼ cups (800ml) chicken stock

4 slices of sourdough baguette

scant ½ cup (50g) grated
  Gruyère cheese

Place a large saucepan over medium heat, add the butter and both onions, and fry, stirring frequently, for 30 to 40 minutes, or until the onions are totally reduced and golden. Add the flour and herbs and cook, stirring constantly, for 2 minutes. Add the wine and bring to a simmer.

Add the stock and cook for another 15 minutes, or until the soup has developed in flavor and the stock has evaporated slightly.

Meanwhile, heat the broiler to high. Toast one side of the baguette slices until golden brown, then flip over and evenly sprinkle the cheese over the top. Place under the broiler and cook until deeply golden.

Ladle the soup into bowls and add the cheese toast so it soaks into the soup. Eat at once.

• •

STORE/MAKE IT VEGAN
For a vegan option, fry the onions in vegan butter, then use vegan cheese and vegetable stock instead of chicken.

This potato soup is very easy—just throw everything into a baking dish and cook. It can be made in advance and reheated before serving.

Spiced new potato soup

with spinach & crispy paneer

PREP TIME: 10 minutes   COOK TIME: 1 hour   SERVES: 2

• •

14 ounces (400g) new potatoes

2 white onions

2½-inch (6cm) piece gingerroot

3 garlic cloves

1 lemon

2 tablespoons ghee

3 tablespoons tikka paste

1 teaspoon chili powder

1 tablespoon mustard seeds

1¾ cups (400ml) coconut milk

14-ounce (400g) can tomatoes

1¾ cups (400ml) vegetable stock

4 cups (200g) baby spinach

7 ounces (200g) paneer cheese

1 handful of cilantro leaves

salt

Preheat the oven to 400°F (200°C).

Chop the potatoes, slice the onions, grate the gingerroot, crush the garlic, and peel and dice the lemon. Add the ghee, onions, garlic, ginger, lemon, and potatoes to a 6 by 8-inch (15 by 20cm) baking dish. Season well with salt and mix well. Roast in the oven for 30 minutes, tossing halfway through.

Remove the tray from the oven, add the tikka paste, chili powder, and mustard seeds, and mix well. Return to the oven for another 10 minutes.

Add the coconut milk, tomatoes, and stock and cook for another 10 minutes. Taste and season with salt.

Add the spinach and paneer, then roast for another 10 minutes, or until the paneer has some color. Ladle into bowls, top with cilantro, and eat at once.

• •

STORE/MAKE IT VEGAN
For a vegan option, swap the paneer for firm tofu and use neutral oil or vegan butter instead of the ghee.

• •

This soup is such a crowd-pleaser as it is so light and refreshing. For a more substantial dinner, serve with some noodles and broiled shrimp.

Carrot & ginger soup

with crispy rice

PREP TIME: 10 minutes   COOK TIME: 26 minutes   SERVES: 2

2 tablespoons coconut oil

4 shallots, chopped

2 garlic cloves, chopped

2½-inch (6cm) piece
   gingerroot, grated

1 lemongrass stalk, chopped

14 ounces (400g)
   carrots, chopped

1 teaspoon ground turmeric

zest and juice of 1 lime

14-ounce (400ml) can
   coconut milk

1 tablespoon fish sauce

¼ cup (60g) Crispy Rice
   (page 178)

1 jalapeño chile, sliced

salt

Heat a medium, heavy saucepan over medium heat, add the oil, shallots, garlic, ginger, and lemongrass, and fry for 8 minutes, stirring frequently.

Add the carrots and turmeric to the pan and fry for another 8 minutes, stirring frequently so nothing catches on the bottom.

Add the lime juice and zest, coconut milk, and one can full of water and simmer for another 10 minutes, or until the carrots are soft. Add the fish sauce, taste, and add a little more, if desired.

Blend the soup with a handheld blender until smooth. Ladle into bowls and top with the crispy rice and fresh jalapeño. Serve at once.

STORE/MAKE IT VEGAN
For a vegan option, simply swap the fish sauce for a vegan fish sauce.

Don't worry if you don't have any homemade stock in the refrigerator or freezer; just buy some good-quality fresh chicken bone broth.

Matzo ball soup

with fresh dill

PREP TIME: 10 minutes   COOK TIME: 55 minutes   SERVES: 2

• •

¾ cup (90g) matzo meal

scant ½ cup (100ml) vegetable oil

3 eggs, whisked

½ teaspoon sea salt

1 tablespoon chopped dill

4¼ cups (1L) chicken stock

2 skinless, boneless chicken
   breasts, 6 ounces (170g) each

juice of ½ lemon

4 carrots, sliced into
   small fingers

1 white onion, cut into 12

2 bay leaves

1 handful of dill leaves

To make the matzo balls, mix the matzo meal, oil, whisked eggs, salt, and chopped dill together in a large bowl until you have a wet dough. Leave the dough in the refrigerator for 30 minutes.

Meanwhile, bring the stock to a simmer in a large saucepan. Add the chicken breasts, lemon juice, carrots, onion, and bay leaves and simmer gently for 10 minutes. Remove the chicken onto a plate and let rest while you cook the broth for another 20 minutes.

Using clean hands, divide the matzo dough into eight equal portions and roll into balls. Fill a medium saucepan with water and bring to a boil. Add the matzo balls, then reduce the heat and simmer for 25 minutes. Scoop the balls out with a slotted spoon and set aside.

Shred the chicken and add to the broth. Ladle into bowls, then divide the matzo balls equally between the bowls and top with dill leaves.

• •

STORE/MAKE IT VEGAN
To store leftover soup, remove the matzo balls and place in an airtight container, then pour the soup into another container. Keep in the refrigerator for up to three days.

• •

These jar soups come into their own when you want to eat healthily at your desk at work or when you are out and about.

Spring in a jar

Spinach, carrot, coconut, turmeric & lentil soup

PREP TIME: 10 minutes   COOK TIME: 5 minutes   SERVES: 2

• •

1 cup (200g) cooked red lentils
    (can also be bought in pouches)
⅓ cup (100g) coconut cream
1 vegetable bouillon cube
1 teaspoon ground turmeric
2 handfuls of spinach
2 carrots, grated

2½-inch (6cm) piece
    gingerroot, grated
1 red chile, chopped
2 makrut lime leaves
1 handful of cilantro leaves
1 handful of mint leaves
1 lime

Divide the lentils between two 27-ounce (750ml) mason jars, then crumble over the coconut cream, bouillon cube, and add ½ teaspoon of turmeric to each.

Top with the spinach, carrots, ginger, red chile, lime leaves, cilantro, and mint, then cover with a lid.

When ready to eat, simply boil a kettle and pour in 1¼ cups (300ml) boiling water. Pop the lid on and let stand for 5 minutes. Uncover and stir well, then squeeze in the juice of half a lime and eat.

• •

STORE/MAKE IT VEGAN
Store the second jar in the refrigerator for a lunch later in the week.

• •

This sums up spring—fresh and bright. If vegan, use vegetable stock and stir in fried spring greens instead of the meatballs.

Lamb meatball soup

with fregola

PREP TIME: 10 minutes   COOK TIME: 30 minutes   SERVES: 2

1 large handful of mint

1 large handful of parsley

1 tablespoon dried oregano

7 ounces (200g) ground lamb

scant 1 cup (50g) breadcrumbs

1 large egg

3 garlic cloves, finely chopped

2 tablespoons olive oil

2 celery stalks, finely diced

1 carrot, finely diced

1 onion, finely diced

1 cup (150g) toasted fregola

1 teaspoon hot pepper flakes

4¼ cups (1L) Beef Bone
    Broth (page 175)

salt and ground black pepper

For the meatballs, chop half the mint and parsley and add to a large bowl with the dried oregano, ground lamb, breadcrumbs, egg, and a third of the chopped garlic. Season with a teaspoon of salt and plenty of black pepper and mix well.
Using clean hands, divide the mixture into 12 portions, then shape each one into walnut-size meatballs. Place on a plate and keep in the refrigerator while you make the soup.

Add the olive oil to a medium saucepan and place over medium heat. Add the remaining garlic, the celery, carrot, and onion and fry for 10 minutes, or until the vegetables are starting to turn soft and a little golden.

Add the fregola and hot pepper flakes and lightly toast for another 2 minutes. Pour in the beef broth and cook for 5 minutes, then add the meatballs and cook for another 10 minutes. Top with the remaining mint and parsley leaves and serve.

STORE/MAKE IT VEGAN
Store leftover soup in an airtight container in the refrigerator for up to three days. Be sure it's cool before storing.

Congee is a traditional Chinese rice soup often eaten with pork or chicken. I use a mix of rice, but you can use just jasmine rice if desired.

Scallion congee

with chile oil & cilantro

PREP TIME: 10 minutes   COOK TIME: 35 to 40 minutes   SERVES: 2

• •

¼ cup (50g) sushi rice

¼ cup (50g) jasmine rice

3 cups (750ml) chicken stock

2 x 2½-inch (6cm) pieces gingerroot, grated

4 garlic cloves, crushed

5 scallions, finely chopped, whites and greens separate

2 large eggs

2 tablespoons toasted sesame seeds

1 handful of cilantro, chopped, and Chile Oil (page 200), for serving

Briefly rinse both types of rice in a colander. There is no need to rinse too much as you want to keep the starch in the rice.

Add the rice to a medium saucepan with the stock and 1 cup (250ml) water. Add the ginger, garlic, and all the white parts of the scallions. Bring to a simmer, then reduce the heat to low and cook for 35 to 40 minutes, stirring frequently to make sure the rice doesn't stick to the bottom of the pan.

When the rice is 10 minutes from being done, bring a small pan of water to a boil. Carefully lower the eggs into the water and boil for 6½ minutes. Drain the eggs and run under cold water until cool enough to handle. Peel the eggs. Tip the sesame seeds onto a plate and roll the eggs around in the seeds until coated all over.

Serve the congee with the eggs, cut in half, the cilantro, chile oil, the greens of the scallions, and any remaining toasted sesame seeds.

• •

STORE/MAKE IT VEGAN
To make this soup vegan, use vegetable stock instead of chicken and omit the eggs.

• •

Three onion soup

with sourdough croutons

PREP TIME: 15 minutes   COOK TIME: 1 hour 5 minutes   SERVES: 2

• •

1 tablespoon olive oil

2 white onions, thinly sliced

2 banana shallots, thinly sliced

2 red onions, thinly sliced

1 stick minus 1 tablespoon (100g)
  unsalted butter

1 small handful of thyme leaves

generous 2 cups (500ml)
  chicken stock

scant ½ cup (100g) crème fraîche

juice of 1 lemon

salt and ground black pepper

1 handful of Sourdough
  Croutons (page 179), for serving

Heat the olive oil in a heavy saucepan over low heat, add the sliced onions and a big pinch of salt, and cook for 10 minutes, or until the onions become translucent.

Add the butter and thyme and cook slowly for another 15 minutes, or until the onions are completely soft. You don't want to take on any browning here.

Add the stock, bring to a boil, then reduce the heat and simmer for 40 minutes. Remove the soup from the heat and add the crème fraîche and lemon juice. Blend the soup with a handheld blender, then season to taste. Ladle into bowls and serve with the croutons.

• •

STORE/MAKE IT VEGAN
For a vegan option, simply swap the chicken stock for vegetable and use vegan butter or spread and vegan crème fraîche.

This feels like a Middle Eastern love letter to beets for me. Store the dukkah in an airtight container in the pantry for up to two months.

Spiced beet soup

with hazelnut dukkah

PREP TIME: 10 minutes   COOK TIME: 55 minutes   SERVES: 2

· ·

2 tablespoons olive oil

2 red onions, coarsely chopped

1 pound 2 ounces (500g) beets, peeled and chopped

1 red chile, diced

2 tablespoons cumin seeds

2 tablespoons coriander seeds

zest and juice of 1 lemon

generous 2 cups (500ml) vegetable stock

⅓ cup (50g) hazelnuts

2 tablespoons sesame seeds

1 teaspoon hot pepper flakes

sea salt

2 tablespoons Greek yogurt, for serving

Add the olive oil to a medium saucepan and place over medium heat. Add the onions, beets, and chile and fry for 15 minutes. Add half the cumin and coriander seeds and toast for a minute, or until aromatic. Add the lemon zest and juice and the stock. Bring to a boil, reduce the heat, cover with a lid, and simmer for 20 minutes.

Meanwhile, make the dukkah. Add the hazelnuts to a large skillet over medium heat and toast until lightly golden. Add the sesame seeds, the remaining cumin and coriander seeds, the hot pepper flakes, and 1 teaspoon salt, and toast, stirring constantly, for 3 minutes, or until deeply aromatic. Blitz the mix briefly in a food processor until coarse. Tip into a bowl—there's no need to clean the food processor.

After 20 minutes, remove the lid from the pan and cook for another 20 minutes, or until the beets are soft when pierced with a knife. Season to taste with salt, then transfer to the processor and blend until smooth.

Ladle into bowls, top with Greek yogurt, and a generous sprinkling of the dukkah.

· ·

STORE/MAKE IT VEGAN
Store any leftover soup in an airtight container in the refrigerator for up to three days.

· ·

This soup is packed full of flavor. If you have Parsley Oil (page 200), then drizzle some over the top at the end. You can make this in advance.

Spanish-style pepper soup

with Manchego croutons

PREP TIME: 10 minutes   COOK TIME: 35 minutes   SERVES: 2

• •

6 Romano or red bell peppers

3½ tablespoons olive oil

4 garlic cloves, sliced

2 onions, sliced into thin moons

1 teaspoon sweet
  smoked paprika

21 ounces (600g) jarred
  cannellini beans

2 tablespoons sherry vinegar

2½ cups (600ml) chicken stock

1 handful of chopped parsley

1 large handful of Sourdough
  Croutons (page 179)

scant ½ cup (50g) grated
  Manchego cheese

salt and ground black pepper

Preheat the broiler to the highest possible heat or preheat a barbecue. Place the peppers under the broiler and char on each side for about 4 minutes, or until black all over. Transfer to a heatproof bowl and cover with plastic wrap or a plate.

Meanwhile, heat the olive oil in a medium saucepan over medium heat. Add the garlic and fry for 4 minutes, stirring, until the garlic is crispy and golden. Using a slotted spoon, remove the garlic from the pan and place on a plate. Add the onions to the pan and fry for 15 minutes, or until sticky and sweet, stirring frequently.

Add the paprika and toast for 30 seconds. Add the beans, vinegar, and stock and reduce the heat to a light simmer. Season to taste with salt and pepper.

Peel the peppers by simply sliding off the skins, then remove the seeds and tear the flesh into strips. Add the pepper strips to the soup and simmer for 10 minutes. Stir through the parsley, then ladle into bowls and top with the reserved crispy garlic, the croutons, and some grated Manchego.

• •

STORE/MAKE IT VEGAN
For a vegan option, simply leave out the cheese and use vegetable stock.

• •

Soup for a crowd

Minestrone

with focaccia

This soup is perfect for a big get-together, as it's not only packed full of goodness but it's hearty and filling, especially if served with homemade focaccia (page 182). If you are vegetarian simply leave out the smoked pancetta and Parmesan and swap the chicken stock for vegetable. This soup is also ideal for using up any leftovers you may have.

SERVING A CROWD: Minestrone

Leftovers can be refrigerated for up to three days and frozen in an airtight container for up to three months. Defrost it fully before reheating.

PREP TIME: 20 minutes   COOK TIME: 40 minutes   SERVES: 6 to 8

• •

scant ½ cup (100ml) olive oil

3½ ounces (100g) diced
 smoked pancetta

4 garlic cloves, sliced

2 white onions, finely chopped

2 fresh bay leaves

3 carrots, cut into
 ½-inch (1cm) dice

3 celery stalks, cut into
 ½-inch (1cm) dice

1 head of kale, shredded

4¼ cups (1L) chicken stock

2 x 14-ounce (400g) cans tomatoes

2 x 14-ounce (400g) cans
 cannellini beans, drained
 and rinsed

juice of 1 lemon

1¼ cups (150g) small dried pasta

To serve
basil leaves
grated Parmesan cheese
Classic Focaccia (page 182)

Heat the olive oil in a large Dutch oven over medium heat. Add the pancetta and fry for 5 minutes, then add the garlic, onions, and bay leaves and fry for another 3 minutes. Add the carrots and celery, reduce the heat to medium to low, and cook for 10 minutes, stirring frequently.

Meanwhile, pull the kale off the woody stems and finely slice the stems. Add the stems to the pot and cook for 10 to 15 minutes until softened and caramelized. Shred the kale leaves and set aside.

Add the chicken stock, tomatoes, and beans and mix well. Add the lemon juice, pasta, and kale leaves, then cover with a lid and simmer for 10 to 15 minutes until the pasta is just cooked.

Serve the minestrone on the table with bowls of basil leaves, grated Parmesan, and chunks of focaccia.

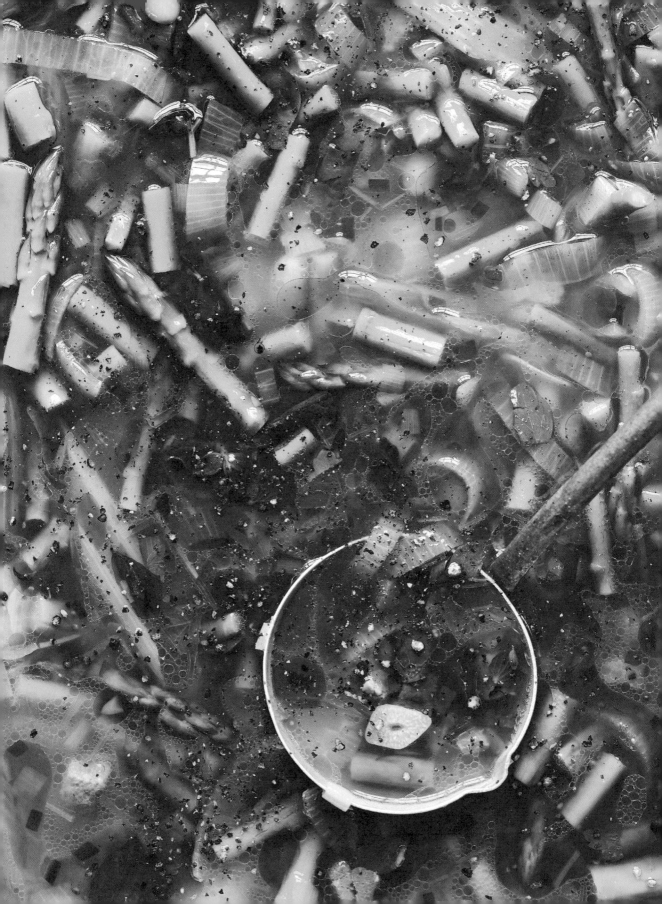

When asparagus is in season I make this soup a lot. I like to finish it with Parsley Oil (page 200), but it is also great without if you don't have any.

Asparagus & white bean soup

with parsley oil

PREP TIME: 10 minutes   COOK TIME: 35 minutes   SERVES: 2

· ·

3½ tablespoons olive oil
3½ ounces (100g) pancetta, diced
4 shallots, chopped
3 garlic cloves, chopped
1 red chile, diced
2 celery stalks, chopped
1 handful of oregano leaves

21 ounces (600g) jarred
   cannellini beans
2⅔ cups (650ml) chicken stock
10½-ounce (300g) bunch
   of asparagus
juice of 1 lemon
1 handful of chopped parsley

salt and ground black pepper
Parsley Oil (page 200), for serving

Add the olive oil to a medium saucepan and place over medium heat. Add the pancetta and fry for 10 minutes, or until starting to turn golden. Add the shallots, garlic, chile, celery, and oregano and fry for 8 to 10 minutes, stirring frequently.

Add the cannellini beans and the liquid they are stored in (if using a can, drain and add a can full of water). Add the stock and simmer for another 10 minutes.

Snap off the woody ends of the asparagus and chop the stems and tips into ¾-inch (2cm) rings, keeping the tips whole. Add to the soup with the lemon juice. Season to taste with salt and pepper, then simmer for another 5 minutes. Add the parsley.

Ladle into bowls and drizzle over the verdant parsley oil.

· ·

STORE/MAKE IT VEGAN
For a vegan option, omit the pancetta and use vegetable stock.

· ·

This Greek-inspired soup is bursting with flavor. You can use any soft green that's in season so feel free to make it your own.

Orzo, lemon & feta soup

with olives & spring greens

PREP TIME: 10 minutes   COOK TIME: 20 minutes   SERVES: 2

• •

4¼ cups (1L) chicken stock
3½ tablespoons olive oil, plus
   extra for drizzling
1 cup (100g) orzo
3 garlic cloves, sliced
generous ¾ cup (100g) chopped
   green olives
juice of 1 lemon

1 head of spring greens,
   finely sliced
⅔ cup (100g) crumbled feta
1 handful of mint, chopped
salt and ground black pepper

Pour the stock into a large saucepan and bring to a boil.

Add the olive oil to a medium saucepan and place over medium heat. Add the orzo and toast until golden. Add the garlic and olives and fry for 1 minute.

Pour in the hot stock, add the lemon juice, and simmer for 10 minutes.

Add the spring greens, half the feta, and half the mint, and simmer for another 5 minutes. Taste and adjust the seasoning. Serve with the remaining feta, mint leaves, and a drizzle of olive oil.

• •

STORE/MAKE IT VEGAN
For a vegan option, swap the chicken stock for vegetable and either omit the feta or use vegan feta.

In spring, carrots are so sweet and full of earthy flavor. You can roast the carrot mix in advance, then blend and reheat when ready to eat.

Carrot & harissa soup

with za'atar

PREP TIME: 10 minutes   COOK TIME: 30 minutes   SERVES: 2

• •

3 tablespoons harissa paste
8 carrots, cut into fingers
1 teaspoon cumin seeds
2 red onions, chopped
1 preserved lemon, chopped
1 red chile, chopped
4 garlic cloves, squashed

generous 2 cups (500ml)
  vegetable stock
1 handful of cilantro leaves
1 tablespoon za'atar
Chile Oil (page 200), for serving

Preheat the oven to 400°F (200°C).

Add the harissa, carrots, cumin seeds, red onions, preserved lemon, chile, and garlic to a high-sided baking pan and roast in the oven for 20 minutes, or until the carrots are sticky and soft to the touch.

Remove the baking pan from the oven and place on the stove over low heat. Using a slotted spoon, remove 3 tablespoons of the carrot mix and set aside.

Add the stock to the baking pan and stir, scraping down the sides of the pan to remove all the sticky bits. Carefully pour the soup mix into a blender or food processor and blend until smooth. Pour into bowls and top with the reserved carrot mix, the cilantro leaves, za'atar, and a drizzle of chile oil.

• •

STORE/MAKE IT VEGAN
Store any leftover soup in an airtight container in the refrigerator for up to three days.

peppers

Peppers have a sweet and mild flavor and partner well with herbs, such as fresh thyme and parsley.

sage

Sage has an earthy and pungent flavor and pairs well with peas, carrots, broccoli, and chicken.

zucchini

Zucchini are in season now and what better way of using up a glut than in a refreshing soup? Try the one on page 91.

fava beans

Young fava beans have a delicate flavor so go well with spring greens. If you have a glut of them, try adding them to a soup.

spinach

As spinach is packed with nutrients, it is a great addition to soups. Use baby spinach leaves.

lettuce

There are lots of varieties of lettuce to choose from in summer, such as Boston lettuce, Bibb, and watercress, as well as baby salad leaves.

potatoes

Try using potatoes in late summer soup recipes as they go well with corn, zucchini, and fennel.

avocado

Avocados have a sweet, nutty taste and a creamy texture, which pairs well with tomatoes, garlic, zucchini, and basil.

celery

Celery has a strong but mild flavor and pairs well with other vegetables, including kale and leeks.

parsley

Fresh parsley has an herbal taste so adding it to soups gives them a greater depth of flavor.

cucumber

Cucumbers are one of the most popular summer foods. They are cooling and are perfect to eat in Gazpacho (page 61) when it's hot.

peas

Fresh peas, especially when young, have a mild, sweet flavor and are the epitome of summer. They go well with mint, lemon, and basil.

tomatoes

Tomatoes are at their best in the summer. They are sweet and flavorful, especially when ripe. They go well with basil, feta, Parmesan, and fennel.

Summer

fennel

Fennel has a delicate anise flavor that goes well with all types of fish and seafood.

snow peas

Snow peas are in season now and make a useful addition to chunky-style soups as they have a sweet, mild flavor. Try the recipe on page 85.

corn

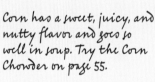

Corn has a sweet, juicy, and nutty flavor and goes so well in soup. Try the Corn Chowder on page 55.

mushrooms

Mushrooms have an earthy and meaty flavor, which goes so well with garlic, cream, crème fraîche, and nuts. Try the recipe on page 59.

onions

Red, yellow, or white onions are perfect for making into soup. They pair well with carrots and bell peppers.

chard

Chard is sweeter than kale. It can be used in much the same way as spinach and is a great addition to chunky soups.

When it's summer and fresh corn is available, I long for this decadent creamy soup. You can add bacon for some extra crunch, if desired.

Corn chowder

with cilantro oil & sliced jalapeños

PREP TIME: 15 minutes   COOK TIME: 25 minutes   SERVES: 2

• •

1 potato
2 ears of corn
¼ stick (30g) unsalted butter
1 white onion, diced
2 garlic cloves, sliced
1 celery stalk, diced
1 small handful of thyme leaves
1 tablespoon all-purpose flour

½ teaspoon sweet
    smoked paprika
⅔ cup (150ml) milk
1 cup (250ml) chicken stock
scant ½ cup (100ml) heavy cream
salt and ground black pepper
sliced jalapeño chiles and
    cilantro oil, for serving

Peel the potato and cut it into ½-inch (1cm) chunks, then husk the corn and slice the kernels from the cob. Set aside.

Add the butter to a medium, heavy saucepan and place over medium heat. Add the onion, garlic, celery, potato, and thyme and fry for 10 minutes, stirring frequently.

Add the flour and paprika and stir around, then stir in the milk. Add the corn and stock and bring to a boil. Reduce the heat to a simmer and cook for 10 minutes, or until the potatoes and corn are tender.

Add the cream and a large pinch of salt and pepper. Blend half the soup with a handheld blender. You want some texture, so be rough when blending.

Taste and adjust the seasoning. Serve with a few slices of jalapeño and cilantro oil.

• •

STORE/MAKE IT VEGAN
For a vegan option, simply swap the chicken stock for vegetable, use vegan spread instead of the butter, and vegan milk and cream instead of the dairy versions.

• •

When it's hot outside, this soup can be eaten as a warm broth rather than a boiling soup. It's so fresh, nourishing, and very filling.

Turkey meatball soup

with fregola & dill

PREP TIME: 10 minutes   COOK TIME: 20 minutes   SERVES: 2

• •

7 ounces (200g) ground turkey

2 garlic cloves, grated

1 teaspoon fennel seeds

1 teaspoon hot pepper flakes

1 handful of chopped parsley

zest and juice of 1 lemon

½ teaspoon flaky sea salt

2 tablespoons olive oil

1 red onion, diced

2 heads of fennel, thinly sliced

1 cup (200g) fregola

3 cups (750ml) chicken stock

1 handful of parsley leaves

1 handful of dill leaves

Start by making the meatballs. Add the ground turkey, garlic, fennel seeds, hot pepper flakes, chopped parsley, the lemon zest, and salt to a large bowl and, using clean hands, mix well. Divide the mixture into about 10 portions and form into walnut-size meatballs. Place the meatballs on a tray and drizzle with 1 tablespoon of the olive oil.

Place a large, heavy saucepan over medium heat and fry the meatballs for a minute on each side until they are colored all over. Remove the meatballs to a plate, then add the remaining olive oil, the onion, sliced fennel, and fregola to the pan and fry for 1 minute.

Add the stock and the meatballs, cover with a lid, and simmer for 15 minutes, or until the fregola is cooked.

Add the lemon juice and herbs and serve.

• •

STORE/MAKE IT VEGAN

Store any leftover soup in an airtight container in the refrigerator for up to three days.

What's not to love about this crispy topped, nutty mushroom soup? Even if you don't love mushrooms, please try this soup, it's so good.

Mushroom soup

with garlic, crème fraîche & chile

PREP TIME: 10 minutes   COOK TIME: 20 minutes   SERVES: 2

• •

½ stick (60g) unsalted butter

3 garlic cloves, sliced

1 pound 5 ounces (600g) mixed
   mushrooms, sliced

1 red chile, diced

zest and juice of 1 lemon

scant 3 cups (700ml)
   vegetable stock

⅔ cup (150g) crème fraîche

salt and ground black pepper

½ bunch of parsley leaves,
   for garnish

Add the butter to a large, heavy saucepan and place over medium heat. Once bubbling, add the garlic and fry until golden. Remove the garlic to a plate.

Add the mushrooms to the pan with the chile and lemon zest and season well with salt. Fry for 8 to 10 minutes until golden and crisp. Remove from the heat and scoop out half the mushrooms with a slotted spoon and set aside. Add half the garlic and the lemon juice to the pan, then pour in the stock and bring to a simmer.

Remove from the heat, add the crème fraîche, and blend with a handheld blender. Taste and adjust the seasoning. Ladle into bowls, top with the reserved mushrooms and garlic and a sprinkling of parsley.

• •

STORE/MAKE IT VEGAN
To make this soup vegan use vegan butter or spread and crème fraîche instead of regular butter and crème fraîche.

This soup is so refreshing and such a joy to eat on those hot, balmy days. You can make it in advance and keep it in the refrigerator.

Gazpacho served on ice

with cucumber, croutons & parsley oil

PREP TIME: 10 minutes   COOK TIME: 2 minutes   SERVES: 2

5 very ripe tomatoes

½ cucumber, chopped

1 green bell pepper, seeded

3½ ounces (100g) stale white bread

1 garlic clove, peeled

1 teaspoon sherry vinegar

1 teaspoon salt

5 tablespoons olive oil

To serve

2 tablespoons diced cucumber

2 tablespoons Rye-Baked
   Crouton Crumb (page 179)

Parsley Oil (page 200)

Have a bowl of cold water ready nearby. Bring a medium saucepan of water to a boil. Using a knife, cut a cross into the base of the tomatoes and drop them into the boiling water.

Using a slotted spoon, scoop out the tomatoes and transfer them to the bowl of cold water. When they are cool enough to handle, peel off the skins.

Add the tomatoes to a blender or food processor with the cucumber, green bell pepper, stale bread, garlic, vinegar, and salt. Add scant 1 cup (200ml) water and blend until smooth. While the blender is on, slowly pour in the olive oil until it is all incorporated.

Pour into bowls and add a handful of ice, the diced cucumber, crouton crumb, and a little parsley oil before serving.

STORE/MAKE IT VEGAN
Keep any leftovers in an airtight container in the refrigerator for up to three days.

This soup is usually made with a whole chicken but I've used chicken breast here for a smaller meal. Use good-quality chicken stock.

Mexican chicken soup

with avocado, cilantro & lime

PREP TIME: 15 minutes   COOK TIME: 45 minutes   SERVES: 2

• •

1 skinless, boneless chicken breast, 9 ounces (250g)

scant 3 cups (700ml) chicken stock

1 red onion, quartered

1 bay leaf

5 garlic cloves

1 teaspoon dried oregano

1 jalapeño chile, sliced

olive oil, for cooking

1 banana pepper, diced

1 large tomato, diced

2 corn tortillas

juice of 2 limes

1 handful of cilantro

1 avocado, sliced

salt

For the soup, add the chicken, stock, onion, bay leaf, three peeled, whole garlic cloves, oregano, and chile to a medium saucepan with scant 1 cup (200ml) of water and simmer gently for 15 to 20 minutes until the chicken is cooked through.

Preheat the oven to 400°F (200°C).

Add 1 tablespoon olive oil, the pepper, tomato, and the remaining two garlic cloves, sliced, to another saucepan and place over medium heat. Fry for 10 minutes, or until soft. Remove the chicken from the soup and set aside. Set a strainer over the vegetables and strain the soup into the vegetables, discarding the bits in the strainer. Let stand over low heat for 10 minutes.

Cut the tortillas into 1¼-inch- (3cm)-long slices, arrange on a baking sheet, and drizzle with oil. Season with salt and roast for 12 minutes, turning halfway through. Shred the chicken and add to soup bowls. Add half the lime juice, taste, and add more if desired. Ladle into the bowls. Top with the tortillas, cilantro, and avocado.

• •

STORE/MAKE IT VEGAN
Keep any leftovers in an airtight container in the refrigerator for up to three days.

• •

This is perfect when fresh peas are at their best as they add a sweetness you need with a spicy broth. Use frozen ones if you can't buy fresh.

Thai green curry

with king shrimp & peas

PREP TIME: 15 minutes   COOK TIME: 20 minutes   SERVES: 2

• •

2½-inch (6cm) piece gingerroot

1 tablespoon peanut oil

3 tablespoons Thai green curry paste

4 makrut lime leaves, torn

14-ounce (400ml) can coconut milk

1¾ cups (400ml) chicken stock

8 large king shrimp, shells on

zest and juice of 1 lime, plus 1 lime cut into wedges

1 tablespoon fish sauce

⅔ cup (100g) fresh peas

7 ounces (200g) cooked rice noodles

1 Thai red chile, sliced

1 handful of Thai basil

Cut the gingerroot into thin matchsticks and set aside. Add the oil and curry paste to a medium saucepan and place over medium heat. Add the ginger and lime leaves and fry for a minute, or until fragrant. Add the coconut milk and stock and reduce to a simmer. Add the shrimp, lime zest and juice, and the fish sauce and simmer for 10 minutes, or until the shrimp are cooked. For the last minute, add the peas.

Divide the cooked noodles between bowls and ladle the soup on top with the red chile and Thai basil. Serve with an extra lime to squeeze over as you eat.

• •

STORE/MAKE IT VEGAN
Store any leftovers in an airtight container in the refrigerator for one to two days, but it's best eaten fresh.

• •

Soup for a crowd

Italian-style fish soup

Italy has many different versions of this simple soup. You can use any seafood you like. Clams and mussels really bulk it out yet are affordable for a gathering. Serve with chilled white wine, lemon wedges, and dollops of aioli for the perfect meal. Close your eyes and imagine you are sitting by the sea in Italy.

SERVING A CROWD: Italian-style fish soup

Best eaten as soon as it's made, but leftovers can be refrigerated for up to two days.

PREP TIME: 20 minutes   COOK TIME: 35 minutes   SERVES: 6 to 8

6 garlic cloves

2 white onions

1 red chile

3 heads of fennel

2¼ pounds (1kg) ripe tomatoes

scant ½ cup (100ml) olive oil

2 small sea bass, about 1¼ pounds
   (600g), chopped into three

1¼ cups (300ml) dry white wine

4¼ cups (1L) fish or
   vegetable stock

12 large shrimp, shells and
   heads on

2¼ pounds (1kg) live mussels
   or clams or a mix

2 lemons

1 bunch of parsley, chopped

salt

Garlic Aioli (page 202) and Classic
   Focaccia (page 182), for serving

Slice the garlic and dice the onions and chile separately. Coarsely chop the fennel, setting the frondy tops aside. Cut the tomatoes into quarters.

Add the olive oil to a large stockpot, then add the garlic, onion, fennel, and chile and sweat over medium heat, stirring frequently for 15 minutes.

Add the tomatoes and fry for another 10 minutes, or until they start to soften a little. Next, add the sea bass, wine, and stock. Cover with a lid and cook for 5 minutes.

Uncover and add the remaining seafood and the juice of one lemon. Cover and cook for another 5 minutes, giving the pan a shake every now and then.

Uncover and add the parsley and reserved fennel fronds. Taste and season with salt. Serve with the remaining lemon, cut into wedges, the aioli, focaccia, and bowls for the empty seafood shells.

This tomato broth is easy to make and is perfect served cold in the summer. You can make this broth in advance and chill for up to two days.

Tomato broth

with tortellini & parsley oil

PREP TIME: 10 minutes/overnight   COOK TIME: 5 minutes   SERVES: 2

• •

2¼ pounds (1kg) ripe tomatoes
1 garlic clove, peeled but whole
1 red chile
1 tablespoon red wine vinegar
1 large handful of basil leaves
10½ ounces (300g) fresh spinach
   and ricotta tortellini

1 tablespoon Parsley Oil
   (page 200)
Parmesan cheese, grated,
   for sprinkling
salt

Add the tomatoes, garlic, red chile, vinegar, and most of the basil to a blender or food processor and blend until smooth.

Place a large piece of cheesecloth over a large bowl and double up the fabric so you have a few layers of cloth. Pour the tomato mix through the cloth. Gather up the sides and make a knot in the top, then hang the cloth bundle on a faucet or in the refrigerator with a bowl underneath. Let stand for a few hours, ideally overnight.

Once all the soup has drained through the cloth, bring a medium saucepan of water to a boil and season with salt. Add the tortellini and cook according to the package directions until al dente.

Ladle the broth into bowls, drain the pasta, and add to the bowls. Top with the remaining basil, a good drizzle of parsley oil, and a grating of Parmesan.

• •

STORE/MAKE IT VEGAN
For a vegan option swap, the spinach and ricotta tortellini for a vegan filled pasta and either omit the Parmesan or use a vegan hard cheese instead.

The combination of sweet corn and poached salmon is a real treat. A dashi broth is used here, but you can use vegetable stock instead.

Salmon & corn broth

with makrut lime & Thai basil

PREP TIME: 10 minutes   COOK TIME: 15 minutes   SERVES: 2

• •

2 ears of corn

2 tablespoons coconut oil

2½-inch (6cm) piece gingerroot,
   cut into matchsticks

1 red chile, sliced

2 garlic cloves, sliced

4 makrut lime leaves

scant 3 cups (700ml) Dashi Broth
   (page 176)

7 ounces (200g) skinless salmon,
   cut into bite-size chunks

1 large handful of spinach leaves

2 scallions, sliced on the bias

1 large handful of Thai basil

Husk the corn and slice the kernels from the cob. Set aside.

Add the oil to a medium saucepan and place over medium heat. Add the ginger, chile, and garlic and fry until golden and crisp.

Add the lime leaves and broth, then reduce the heat to a simmer. Add the salmon and cook for 5 minutes. Add the corn and spinach and cook for another 5 minutes.

Ladle into bowls and top with sliced scallions and Thai basil.

• •

STORE/MAKE IT VEGAN
Keep any leftovers in an airtight container in the refrigerator for up to three days. For best results, reheat over medium heat until hot.

This fava bean soup is so simple to make. If you have a Parmesan rind, add it to the soup for extra flavor. Serve with focaccia (page 182).

Italian fava bean broth

with pancetta & mint

PREP TIME: 5 minutes   COOK TIME: 25 minutes   SERVES: 2

• •

3½ tablespoons olive oil
2 garlic cloves, sliced
1 red onion, diced
3½ ounces (100g) pancetta, diced
½ red chile, diced
1¼ cups (300ml) white wine
10½ ounces (300g) fava
   beans, shelled

zest and juice of 1 lemon
1 handful of mint, chopped, plus
   extra for serving
generous 2 cups (500ml)
   chicken stock
grated Pecorino Romano,
   for serving

Add the olive oil to a medium saucepan, then add the garlic and onion and fry for a few minutes. Add the pancetta and chile and fry for another 10 minutes, or until the pancetta is golden.

Add the wine and fava beans, followed by the lemon zest and juice. Add the mint and stock and cook for another 10 minutes.

Ladle into bowls and serve with a little extra mint and grated cheese.

• •

STORE/MAKE IT VEGAN
Store any leftovers in an airtight container in the refrigerator for up to three days.

• •

This soup is perfect when tomatoes are at their very best. Before serving, drizzle with some extra olive oil, if desired.

Roasted tomato soup

with sourdough croutons & capers

PREP TIME: 10 minutes   COOK TIME: 55 minutes   SERVES: 2

• •

1¾ pounds (800g) ripe
   tomatoes, halved
6 garlic cloves, skins on
   and smashed
1 onion, cut into 8 wedges
1 small handful of oregano
2 tablespoons capers, drained
¼ cup (60ml) olive oil

3 cups (750ml) chicken stock
2 large handfuls of Sourdough
   Croutons page (179)
1 tablespoon red wine vinegar
1 handful of basil leaves
salt and ground black pepper

Preheat the oven to 400°F (200°C).

Add the tomatoes, garlic, onion, oregano leaves, and capers to a high-sided baking sheet and drizzle over the olive oil. Season with salt and pepper and roast in the oven for 45 minutes.

Add everything from the baking sheet to a large saucepan, removing and discarding the garlic skins. Pour in the stock, half the croutons, the vinegar, and most of the basil leaves and simmer for 10 minutes.

Blend most or all of the soup (this bit is up to you), then divide between bowls and top with the reserved croutons and basil leaves.

• •

STORE/MAKE IT VEGAN
For a vegan option, swap the chicken stock with vegetable stock.

• •

Chard & pasta soup

with chickpeas

PREP TIME: 10 minutes   COOK TIME: 25 minutes   SERVES: 2

• •

21 ounces (600g) jarred chickpeas

juice of 1 lemon

3 tablespoons olive oil

1 carrot, diced

1 onion, diced

1 celery stalk, diced

4 garlic cloves, sliced

1 handful of rosemary, chopped

1 bay leaf

4 tomatoes, coarsely chopped

½ teaspoon hot pepper flakes

generous 2 cups (500ml)
    chicken stock

scant 1 cup (90g) macaroni

3½ ounces (100g) Swiss chard

salt and ground black pepper

Add half the chickpeas with half of the liquid they are stored in to a blender or food processor. Add the lemon juice and blend until smooth.

Place a medium saucepan over medium heat, add the olive oil, carrot, onion, celery, garlic, rosemary, and bay leaf and fry for 10 minutes, or until soft.

Add the tomatoes, hot pepper flakes, blended chickpeas, the remaining chickpeas, and the chicken stock to the pan and bring to a boil. Add the macaroni and cook for 10 minutes.

Tear the chard leaves off the stems and finely slice the stems. Add the stems to the soup, then coarsely shred the leaves, add them to the pan, and cook for the last few minutes. Taste and season with salt and pepper.

• •

STORE/MAKE IT VEGAN
For a vegan option, swap the chicken stock for vegetable stock.

There are numerous versions of gumbo, so once you have mastered this one, try using fish, chicken, and other seafood.

Shrimp gumbo

with parsley

PREP TIME: 15 minutes   COOK TIME: 30 minutes   SERVES: 2

• •

8 large shrimp

5½ ounces (150g) okra

1 green bell pepper, seeded

2 tablespoons olive oil

1 onion, chopped

2 celery stalks, sliced

2 green jalapeño chiles, sliced

4 garlic cloves, finely chopped

2 chorizo sausages, sliced

4 tomatoes, chopped

1 small bunch of thyme, stemmed

2 tablespoons all-purpose flour

2½ cups (600ml) chicken stock

1 teaspoon sweet paprika

1 handful of parsley, chopped

salt and ground black pepper

Remove the heads and veins from the shrimp, but keep the tails and set aside. Slice the okra into ½-inch (1cm) rings. Set aside. Chop the green bell pepper into pieces.

Heat the olive oil in a heavy saucepan over medium heat, add the onion, celery, bell pepper, chiles, and garlic and fry for 10 minutes, or until softened. Add the chorizo and okra and fry for 6 to 8 minutes until browned. Add the tomatoes and thyme and fry for another 5 minutes.

Using a slotted spoon, scoop the vegetables and chorizo mix out of the pan into a clean bowl, leaving the oil behind, and set aside. Add the flour to the oil and fry until the flour turns a golden color. Slowly add the stock, whisking as you go, then add the paprika and season with salt and pepper.

Add the vegetable mix back to the pan, followed by the shrimp and most of the parsley. Simmer for 6 minutes, or until the shrimp are cooked. Sprinkle the remaining parsley over the top and serve.

• •

STORE/MAKE IT VEGAN
For a vegan option, omit the shrimp and chorizo and use a mix of different colored bell peppers. Substitute the chicken stock with vegetable.

• •

I've based this soup on Elote, a grilled Mexican street corn dish. Add some broiled jumbo shrimp for a bigger meal.

Elote-style corn soup

with tortillas, jalapeños & cotija cheese

PREP TIME: 10 minutes   COOK TIME: 20 minutes   SERVES: 2

• •

4 ears of corn
2 tablespoons olive oil
1 tablespoon unsalted butter
1 onion, diced
3 garlic cloves, thinly sliced
1 teaspoon chili powder
2 teaspoons ground cumin
¼ teaspoon ground coriander

2 teaspoons smoked paprika
generous 2 cups (500ml)
  chicken stock
zest and juice of 1 lime
scant ½ cup (100ml) heavy cream
2 tortillas, cut into strips and
  fried until crisp
2 jalapeño chiles, sliced

¼ cup (25g) grated cotija cheese
salt and ground black pepper

Husk the corn and slice the kernels from the cob. Set aside.

Add the olive oil and butter to a medium saucepan and place over medium heat. Add the onion and fry for 5 minutes, or until soft and just starting to color. Add the garlic and all the spices and fry for another few minutes, stirring constantly.

Increase the heat to medium to high, add the corn kernels, and cook for 5 minutes, stirring constantly so nothing sticks and burns.

Add half the corn mixture to a blender or food processor along with half the stock and the lime zest and juice and blend until smooth and creamy.

Pour the blended soup back into the pan with the remaining stock and stir. Season to taste with salt and pepper. Reduce the heat to low and simmer for 5 minutes. Stir in the cream.

Ladle into bowls and top with fried tortillas, chiles, and grated cheese.

• •

STORE/MAKE IT VEGAN
For a vegan option, use vegetable stock instead of chicken, swap the butter and heavy cream for vegan versions, and make sure all the toppings are vegan.

• •

Serve this summery laksa with Crispy Onions (page 178), cilantro leaves, lime wedges, and bean sprouts.

Chicken laksa

with snow peas

PREP TIME: 15 minutes   COOK TIME: 20 minutes   SERVES: 2

• •

2½-inch (6cm) piece gingerroot, peeled

2 skinless, boneless chicken breasts, 6 ounces (170g) each

1 tablespoon peanut oil

1 tablespoon sesame oil

1 lemongrass stalk, chopped

3 scallions, sliced

2 garlic cloves, finely chopped

2 red chiles, finely chopped

generous 2 cups (500ml) chicken stock

14-ounce (400ml) can coconut milk

juice of 1 lime

2 tablespoons fish sauce

1 tablespoon tomato paste

2 teaspoons peanut butter

1 teaspoon soft brown sugar

½ teaspoon ground turmeric

1 large handful of snow peas

7 ounces (200g) rice noodles, cooked

Finely grate the gingerroot. Coarsely chop the chicken and set aside.

Heat the oils in a medium saucepan over medium heat. Add the lemongrass, scallions, garlic, grated gingerroot, and chiles and fry for 2 minutes.

Add the reserved chicken, increase the heat to high, and cook for another 5 minutes. Pour in the stock, coconut milk, and lime juice and bring to a simmer.

Add the fish sauce, tomato paste, peanut butter, sugar, and turmeric and simmer gently for 10 minutes. For the last minute, add the snow peas.

Divide the cooked noodles between serving bowls, ladle in the soup, and top with toppings of choice.

• •

STORE/MAKE IT VEGAN
Store leftovers in an airtight container in the refrigerator for up to three days. If there are any noodles, then scoop them out and store in another container.

This soup is very refreshing on a hot day. If you are feeling particularly hungry, you can serve with rice or noodles, if desired.

Sweet & sour soup

with spiced fish balls

PREP TIME: 10 minutes   COOK TIME: 15 minutes   SERVES: 2

· ·

10½ ounces (300g) firm white fish, we used cod, coarsely chopped

3 lemongrass stalks, 1 coarsely chopped and 2 lightly crushed

2 large handfuls of cilantro

6 makrut lime leaves

3 red chiles, thinly sliced

2 tablespoons fish sauce

generous 2 cups (500ml) chicken stock

2½-inch (6cm) piece galangal, peeled and sliced

8 tomatoes, cut into quarters,

1 tablespoon tamarind paste

1 tablespoon soft brown sugar

1 small bunch of Thai basil leaves, for garnish

2 limes, halved, for serving

Add the fish chunks to a food processor, with the coarsely chopped lemongrass stalk, most of the cilantro leaves, keeping the stems for the broth, two lime leaves, one red chile, and 1 tablespoon of the fish sauce and blitz until the mixture forms an almost smooth consistency. Scoop the mixture out and form into 12 walnut-size balls. Place on a plate and let chill in the refrigerator.

Pour the stock into a medium saucepan, add scant 1 cup (200ml) water, and bring to a boil over medium heat. Add the remaining lemongrass, the cilantro stems, galangal, tomatoes, remaining lime leaves, the rest of the fish sauce and red chiles, the tamarind, and sugar to the pan. Reduce the heat and simmer for 10 minutes.

Add the fish balls, reduce the heat to low, and poach for 5 minutes. Ladle into bowls, top with Thai basil, and serve with lime.

· ·

STORE/MAKE IT VEGAN
Keep leftovers in an airtight container in the refrigerator for up to three days. If there are any fish balls, then scoop them out and store in another container.

Summer vegetables are so sweet-tasting and this soup brings out their flavors. Use spiralized sweet potato for a more substantial lunch.

Summer in a jar

Peas, fennel, tomato, miso & zucchini noodle soup

PREP TIME: 10 minutes   COOK TIME: 2 minutes   SERVES: 2

• •

2 medium zucchini
1 handful of fresh peas, shelled
1 head of fennel, diced
2 handfuls of cherry
   tomatoes, halved
¾ cup (160g) kernels from 1 ear
   of corn

1 large handful of Thai
   basil leaves
2 tablespoons white miso
2 tablespoons Chile Oil
   (page 200)

Using a spiralizer simply spiralize the zucchini into noodles—don't worry if they break a little. Divide them between two 27-ounce (750ml) jars.

Top the noodles with a layer of peas, fennel, tomatoes, corn, and basil leaves.

Mix the miso and chile oil together to form a thick paste. Spoon into the jars, cover with a lid, and keep in the refrigerator until needed.

When ready to eat, pour over 1½ cups (350ml) boiling water, mix well, and enjoy.

• •

STORE/MAKE IT VEGAN
Keep the other jar in the refrigerator for lunch for later in the week.

You can use whatever vegetable is in season in this stew, or you can add greens for more versatility. Serve with focaccia (page 183).

Zucchini & bean stew

with a chopped herb oil

PREP TIME: 15 minutes   COOK TIME: 30 minutes   SERVES: 2

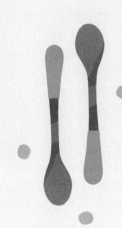

2 medium zucchini

3½ tablespoons olive oil

1 leek, sliced

1 onion, sliced

1 handful of sage, shredded

2 garlic cloves, sliced

1 teaspoon fennel seeds

zest and juice of 1 lemon

1¼ cups (300ml) white wine

14-ounce (400g) can lima beans, drained and rinsed

1¼ cups (300ml) vegetable stock

⅔ cup (100g) fresh peas

2 tablespoons Chopped Herb Oil (page 201)

salt

Cut the zucchini into ½-inch (1cm) chunks. Set aside.

Add the olive oil to a medium saucepan, add the sliced leek and onion, and fry for 10 minutes, or until sticky and reduced.

Season with salt, then add the sage and garlic and fry for another 5 minutes. Add the zucchini and fennel seeds and fry for 5 minutes.

Add the lemon zest and juice, then pour in the wine and let the wine evaporate for a few minutes before adding the beans and stock. Simmer for another 10 minutes. For the last few minutes of cooking time, add the peas.

Ladle into bowls, drizzle with the herb oil, and serve.

STORE/MAKE IT VEGAN
Keep any leftovers in an airtight container in the refrigerator for up to three days.

pumpkin

As pumpkins have a sweet flavor, they partner well with strong spices and coconut milk to make filling soups.

celery root

Celery root, or celeriac, is a root vegetable that's harvested in fall and winter. It has a distinctive taste—nutty and sweet with a celery flavor.

celery

Celery has a strong but mild flavor and makes a good addition to warming soups alongside kale and leeks. Try the recipe on page 101.

arugula

As arugula has a peppery flavor, it makes a great soup, especially if it's combined with cheese and a fruity olive oil.

chard

Chard, or Swiss chard, is sweeter than kale. It is a great addition to chunky-style soups.

scallions

Scallions are sweeter and milder than regular onions and go well with leeks, peas, and squash.

potatoes

The best potato to use for soup are either Russet or Yukon Gold as they soak up the broth and lose their shape.

leeks

Leeks have a mild, sweet flavor, which goes well with other foods that we associate with fall, such as potatoes, mushrooms, and thyme.

sweetheart cabbage

There are many varieties of cabbage but green cabbage has a sweet, slightly spicy flavor when cooked. Try the Korean Kimchi soup on page 131.

Brussels sprouts

Brussels sprouts are available right through until March. They have a nutty flavor and are great paired with lime.

radishes

Ranging from mild to hot and peppery to pungent, there are lots of varieties of radish to choose from in the fall and winter.

carrots

Carrots are very versatile as they have a sweet flavor, so they pair well with most soup ingredients (see page 117).

broccoli

You can use both the florets and stems in soups, which can help to reduce food waste.

kale

Tuscan kale is in season and is a great addition to soups, such as the classic Italian soup Ribollita on page 129.

Fall

squash

There are so many varieties of squash available in the fall. Their earthy and nutty taste pairs well with mushrooms and lentils.

parsnips

Parsnips have a sweet, earthy, and slightly peppery flavor and make wonderful soups. Try the Creamy Parsnip Soup on page 103.

tomatoes

By fall tomatoes are bursting with flavor and partner well with hearty lentils, beans, squash, pumpkin, carrots, herbs, and cheese.

apples

Adding apples to soup gives the soup a sweet taste that goes so well with other savory flavors.

Roasted squash dal

with turmeric & ginger

PREP TIME: 20 minutes   COOK TIME: 30 minutes   SERVES: 2

• •

1 small acorn or kuri squash

1 tablespoon coconut oil

4 garlic cloves, grated

2½-inch (6cm) piece
  gingerroot, grated

2 Indian green chiles, halved

1 large onion, diced

1 tablespoon curry powder

1 teaspoon ground turmeric

14-ounce (400ml) can
  coconut milk

zest and juice of 1 lemon

½ cup (100g) red lentils

3 tablespoons Indian Curry Leaf
  & Seed Oil (page 201)

salt and ground black pepper

Preheat the oven to 400°F (200°C).

Seed and coarsely chop the squash into curved slices, then add to a high-sided baking pan with the coconut oil, garlic, gingerroot, chiles, onion, curry powder, and turmeric. Using two metal spoons, toss everything together, then roast in the oven for 10 minutes, tossing halfway through.

Remove from the oven, then pour in the coconut milk plus a can of water. Add the lemon zest and juice and the lentils. Cover with foil and roast for another 20 minutes, or until the lentils are cooked through.

Transfer half of the lentil mix to a blender or food processor and blend, then stir it back through the baking pan. Taste and season to your liking, adding a little extra water, if needed. Drizzle with the Indian seed oil and serve.

• •

STORE/MAKE IT VEGAN
Keep any leftovers in an airtight container in the refrigerator for up to five days. As this soup keeps very well, make a double batch to eat through the week.

• •

This classic soup is simple to make. The celery root adds a nutty, creamy flavor through the smoky fish.

Smoked haddock soup

with celery root

PREP TIME: 20 minutes   COOK TIME: 30 to 35 minutes   SERVES: 2

••

3½ tablespoons unsalted butter

2 tablespoons olive oil

2 leeks, finely sliced

14 ounces (400g) celery root, peeled and diced

2 potatoes, diced

1 cup (250ml) fish or vegetable stock

2 handfuls of spring greens, shredded

1¼ cups (300ml) milk

9 ounces (250g) undyed smoked haddock, skinless and chopped into 1¼-inch (3cm) chunks

1 bay leaf

1 large handful of flat-leaf parsley

salt and ground black pepper

Parsley Oil (page 200), for serving

Heat the butter and olive oil in a medium saucepan, add the leeks with a good pinch of salt, and gently fry for 10 minutes, or until soft.

Add the celery root and potatoes and cook for 5 minutes. Add the stock, bring to a boil, and cook for 5 to 10 minutes until the potatoes are cooked. Add the greens and fry for another 5 minutes.

Pour in the milk, then add the fish and bay leaf and simmer for 5 minutes.

Stir in most of the parsley, season to taste, and serve with parsley oil.

••

STORE/MAKE IT VEGAN
Keep any leftovers in an airtight container in the refrigerator for up to three days.
Make sure it's fully cool before storing.

••

This spiced soup is sweet but with a punch from a habanero chile. If you don't like too much spice, omit the chile or swap it for a long red chile.

Pumpkin spiced soup

with buttery nuts

PREP TIME: 10 minutes   COOK TIME: 25 minutes   SERVES: 2

• •

1¼ pounds (600g) pumpkin

2 tablespoons groundnut oil

6 garlic cloves, smashed

1 red onion, chopped

2 celery stalks, chopped

½ habanero chile

1 teaspoon ground ginger

1 teaspoon ground cinnamon

½ teaspoon ground allspice

3½ tablespoons butter

¾ cup (100g) mixed
    nuts, chopped

scant 1 cup (200ml) canned
    coconut milk

1¼ cups (300ml) chicken stock

salt

Preheat the oven to 400°F (200°C).

Seed the pumpkin and cut the flesh into bite-size pieces, then add to a large baking pan with the oil, garlic, onion, celery, habanero, half of the spices, and a good pinch of salt and toss it all together. Roast for 20 minutes, mixing halfway through.

Add the butter to a large skillet and add the nuts. Place over medium heat and toss them all about until the butter is brown and the nuts are golden. For the last minute, add the remaining spices, toss, and remove from the heat.

Once the vegetables are cooked, tip them into a blender or food processor with the coconut milk and stock and blend until smooth. Pour into a pan and heat gently until hot. Ladle into bowls and top with the buttery nuts.

• •

STORE/MAKE IT VEGAN
For a vegan option, substitute the chicken stock with vegetable stock and use vegan butter to fry the nuts.

Traditionally, this soup is made with beef or lamb, but personally, I like this lighter version. Serve with the yogurt flatbreads on page 186.

Celery & white bean soup

with crunchy toppings

PREP TIME: 10 minutes   COOK TIME: 40 minutes   SERVES: 2

• •

3 tablespoons olive oil, plus
    extra for serving
2 onions, diced
10½ ounces (300g) celery, stalks
    separated, trimmed and cut into
    1¼-inch (3cm) lengths
3 garlic cloves, minced
1 teaspoon ground turmeric

1 preserved lemon, diced
2 tablespoons tomato paste
1 bunch of parsley, chopped
21 ounces (600g) jarred
    cannellini or haricot beans
1 handful of mint leaves, chopped
Speedy Yogurt Flatbreads (page
    187), for serving

Add the olive oil to a medium saucepan and place over medium heat. Add the onions and fry for 10 minutes. Add the celery and garlic and fry for another 10 minutes. Add the turmeric, preserved lemon, tomato paste, and most of the parsley and cook for a minute.

Add the beans and the liquid they are stored in, then fill the jar with water and add the water to the pan as well. Simmer for 15 minutes.

Add most of the mint and simmer for another 5 minutes.

Ladle into bowls and top with extra olive oil and the remaining mint and parsley. Serve at once with flatbreads.

• •

STORE/MAKE IT VEGAN
Keep any leftovers in an airtight container in the refrigerator for up to three days.

Creamy parsnip soup

with Gruyère croutons

PREP TIME: 15 minutes   COOK TIME: 30 minutes   SERVES: 2

1 pound (450g) parsnips
3 tablespoons olive oil
1 tablespoon butter
2 garlic cloves, finely chopped
1 tablespoon honey
1 small bunch of thyme,
  leaves picked

1 teaspoon hot pepper flakes,
4¼ cups (1L) hot
  vegetable stock
2 thick slices sourdough
⅔ cup (70g) finely grated
  Gruyère cheese
6 sage leaves, shredded

scant 1 cup (200ml) heavy cream
⅓ cup (50g) toasted
  hazelnuts, chopped
salt and ground black pepper

Peel and cut the parsnips into ¾-inch (2cm) chunks. Heat 1 tablespoon of the olive oil and the butter in a heavy saucepan over medium heat. Add the garlic, parsnips, and honey and fry for 5 minutes, stirring occasionally, until colored. Add the thyme and hot pepper flakes and fry for 1 minute. Pour in the stock, stir, and bring to a simmer. Cover with the lid and cook for 15 minutes, or until the parsnips are soft when prodded with a fork.

Meanwhile, preheat the oven to 400°F (200°C).

Tear the bread into bite-size chunks, spread out on a baking sheet in a single layer, and drizzle with the remaining oil. Sprinkle over the cheese and sage, then season with salt and pepper. Bake for 10 minutes, or until crisp and golden.

Remove the soup from the heat and blitz with a stick blender until smooth. Return to the heat, stir in the cream, and heat through. Season to taste, then divide between bowls and top with the croutons and hazelnuts.

STORE/MAKE IT VEGAN
Keep any leftover soup, without the croutons and hazelnuts, in an airtight container in the refrigerator for up to three days. Or freeze for up to three months.

Serve this earthy green soup with my rye crouton crumb (page 179), but if you don't have time, croutons or a slice of warm bread works well too.

Broccoli & ricotta soup

with toasted pine nuts & a rye-baked crouton crumb

PREP TIME: 10 minutes   COOK TIME: 20 minutes   SERVES: 2

• •

3½ tablespoons olive oil
1 onion, diced
1 leek, finely sliced
3 garlic cloves, sliced
1 red chile, diced
1 head of broccoli, about
  ¾ pound (350g), chopped
zest and juice of 1 lemon

1¾ cups (400ml) vegetable stock
⅔ cup (150g) ricotta
⅓ cup (50g) toasted pine nuts
Rye-Baked Crouton Crumb
  (page 179)

Add the olive oil to a medium saucepan and place over medium heat. Add the onion and leek and fry for 10 minutes. Add the garlic, red chile, broccoli, and lemon zest and juice and fry for another 10 minutes, stirring frequently.

Pour in the stock, then add most of the ricotta. Bring to a simmer, then, using a stick blender, blend until velvety smooth.

Ladle into bowls and top with the remaining ricotta, the roasted pine nuts, and some crouton crumb.

• •

STORE/MAKE IT VEGAN
For a vegan option, use vegan ricotta instead of dairy ricotta.

• •

This sweet, creamy, spiced soup is a winner. If you are vegetarian, simply swap the stock; if you aren't a fan of chile, simply leave it out.

Celery root soup

with hazelnuts & sage

PREP TIME: 10 minutes   COOK TIME: 45 minutes   SERVES: 2

• •

2 tablespoons olive oil
2 tablespoons butter
2 garlic cloves, sliced
1 red chile, thinly sliced
15 sage leaves
½ pound (225g) celery root
1 cooking apple

2 onions, diced
1 celery stalk, diced
1 tablespoon white wine vinegar
a few sprigs of thyme
generous 2 cups (500ml)
   chicken stock
scant ½ cup (100g) Greek yogurt

¾ cup (100g) toasted
   hazelnuts, chopped
salt

Add the oil and butter to a medium saucepan and place over medium heat. Add the garlic and red chile and fry until the garlic is golden and crisp. Remove with a slotted spoon onto a plate. Next, add the sage leaves and fry until crisp. Remove from the pan and set aside.

Peel and cut the celery root into bite-size pieces, then peel, core, and coarsely chop the apple. Set aside.

Put the pan over medium heat, add the onions, and fry for 5 minutes. Add the celery, celery root, apple, vinegar, and thyme and fry for another 5 minutes.

Pour in the stock and simmer for 25 minutes. Season to taste with salt. Add half of the reserved chile, garlic, and sage, along with the yogurt and half the hazelnuts. Using a stick blender, blend until smooth.

Ladle into bowls and top with the remaining fried chile, garlic, sage, and hazelnuts.

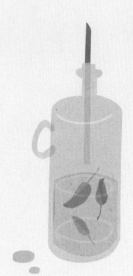

• •

STORE/MAKE IT VEGAN
To make this soup vegan, use vegan butter or spread, substitute the chicken stock for vegetable, and swap the Greek yogurt for a non-dairy one.

• •

This Irish beef and Guinness stew is a simple, hearty classic. It freezes really well, so double up the recipe and freeze it for a rainy day.

Irish beef soup

with Guinness

PREP TIME: 10 minutes   COOK TIME: 3½ hours   SERVES: 2

• •

1 pound 2 ounces (500g)
  beef chuck
2 russet potatoes
2 carrots
3 tablespoons extra-virgin olive oil
1 onion, chopped
2 celery stalks, chopped

3 garlic cloves, sliced
1 small handful of thyme leaves
2 bay leaves
generous 2 cups
  (500ml) Guinness
generous 2 cups (500ml) Beef
  Bone Broth (page 175)

2 tablespoons tomato paste
2 tablespoons
  Worcestershire sauce
salt and ground black pepper

Cut the beef into bite-size pieces, then peel the potatoes and cut them into large chunks. Peel the carrots and cut them into circles. Set aside.

Place a large, heavy saucepan over medium heat. Season the beef generously with salt and pepper, then add to the pan with the oil and fry on all sides until taking on some good color, about 15 minutes. Transfer the beef to a plate and set aside.

Add the onion, carrots, and celery to the pan and cook, stirring frequently, until soft. Add the garlic and cook for a minute. Add the thyme and bay leaves and fry for another minute.

Pour in the Guinness and let the alcohol evaporate for a moment. Add the broth and the reserved beef. Add the tomato paste and Worcestershire sauce and bring to a boil. Reduce the heat, cover with a lid, and simmer for 2 hours, stirring occasionally.

Add the reserved potatoes and simmer for another hour. Season to taste and serve.

• •

STORE/MAKE IT VEGAN
Keep any leftover soup in an airtight container in the refrigerator for up to three days. Or freeze for up to three months. Defrost and heat until piping hot.

• •

Fall in a jar

Instant noodles, kimchi, scallions & cabbage soup

PREP TIME: 10 minutes   COOK TIME: 5 minutes   SERVES: 2

• •

2½-inch (6cm) piece
   gingerroot, grated

1 garlic clove, grated

2 tablespoons tamari

2 x 3½-ounce (100g) packages
   spicy ramen noodles or instant
   noodles of your choice

3½ ounces (100g) kimchi

2 handfuls of shredded
   napa cabbage

3 scallions, sliced

Add the ginger and garlic to the bottom of two 25-ounce (750ml) mason jars, then pour over the tamari.

Break the noodles into the jars and top with a layer of kimchi, shredded cabbage, and top with the scallions.

When ready to eat, empty the flavor sachet that comes with the noodles and pour over 1¼ cups (300ml) boiling water. Pop the lid on and let stand for 5 minutes. Mix well and enjoy.

• •

STORE/MAKE IT VEGAN
Store the second jar in the refrigerator for a lunch later in the week.

I love sticky, sweet, and spiced roast squash when in season. Be sure to scrape the baking pan, adding all the bits into the bowl as you serve.

Roasted squash broth

with egg noodles

PREP TIME: 15 minutes   COOK TIME: 25 minutes   SERVES: 2

• •

1¼ pounds (600g) acorn
  or butternut squash
1 tablespoon coconut oil
1 handful of cherry
  tomatoes, halved
1 teaspoon Chinese 5 spice
3 garlic cloves, sliced
1 lemongrass stalk, bashed

4 star anise
scant 3 cups (700ml) Dashi
  Broth (page 176)
2½-inch (6cm) piece
  gingerroot, peeled and grated
2 nests of medium egg noodles,
  1¾ ounces (50g) per nest
salt

Preheat the oven to 400°F (200°C).

Seed and cut the squash into thin boats.

Add the coconut oil to a baking pan and tumble in the sliced squash, tomatoes, 5 spice, and sliced garlic. Season with salt and roast in the oven for 20 minutes, flipping halfway through.

Meanwhile, place a medium saucepan over medium heat. Add the lemongrass and star anise and toast for a minute. Pour in the broth and add the grated ginger. Let simmer over low heat.

Cook the noodles according to the package directions, then run under cold water.

Divide the noodles between two bowls, ladle in the broth, and top with the roasted vegetable mixture. Serve.

• •

STORE/MAKE IT VEGAN
Store any leftover soup, without the noodles, in an airtight container in the refrigerator for up to three days. Store the egg noodles separately.

Soup for a crowd

..

Chicken noodle soup

with parsley & celery

This has to be one of my desert island dishes. The soup is packed full of flavor for such little effort and is the perfect fall dinner party dish to serve everyone. After the chicken thighs have been fried, the skin is removed and then crisped up in the oven for a salty little crunch at the end. Serve with warm bread and extra lemon wedges, if desired.

SERVING A CROWD: Chicken noodle soup

Serve the soup on the table with chopped parsley, the reserved celery leaves, and the chicken skin to crumble over.

PREP TIME: 20 minutes   COOK TIME: 55 minutes   SERVES: 6 to 8

¼ cup (60ml) olive oil

10 chicken thighs, skin on and
   bone in, about 5 ounces
   (140g) each

2 onions, diced

4 carrots, coarsely diced

4 celery stalks, diced and
   leaves reserved

6 garlic cloves, sliced

4 rosemary stalks

juice of 2 lemons

10 cups (2.5L) chicken stock

7 ounces (200g) vermicelli egg
   noodles, snapped in half

1 head of kale, shredded

1 handful of parsley, chopped

flaky sea salt

Add the olive oil to a large, heavy saucepan and place over high heat. Season the chicken with sea salt, then place the chicken in the pan, skin-side down, and fry for 6 to 8 minutes until the skin is golden and crisp. Flip the chicken and fry on the other side for a few minutes. Remove the chicken to a plate.

Add the onions, carrots, and celery to the pan, reduce the heat to medium, and fry for 10 minutes, or until soft. Add the garlic and rosemary and fry for 5 minutes.

Preheat the oven to 350°F (180°C). Remove the skin from the chicken and place on a baking sheet lined with baking parchment.

Add the lemon juice and stock to the pan and add the chicken. Bring to a boil, then reduce the heat and simmer for 20 minutes.

Roast the chicken skin for 10 minutes, or until crispy. Remove and set aside.

When the soup is done, remove the chicken. Add the noodles and kale and cook for 10 minutes. Shred the chicken off the bone and add the meat to the soup. Taste and season with extra salt, if needed.

This soup is very versatile as you can use any greens and top it with anything you fancy. You can also swap the broth for chicken stock.

Miso & ginger ramen

with quick pickled radish

PREP TIME: 10 minutes   COOK TIME: 20 minutes   SERVES: 2

• •

1 cup (250ml) rice wine vinegar

2 tablespoons sea salt

1 tablespoon sugar

1 jalapeño chile, sliced

1 watermelon radish, thinly sliced

2½-inch (6cm) piece gingerroot

7 ounces (200g) Swiss chard

2 large eggs

1 tablespoon sesame wok oil

2 garlic cloves, sliced

1 tablespoon crispy chile oil

2 nests of ramen noodles,
   1¾ ounces (50g) each nest

scant 3 cups (700ml) Dashi Broth
   (page 176)

2 tablespoons white miso

For the pickled radish, add the vinegar and 1 cup (250ml) water to a small saucepan, then add the salt, sugar, and jalapeño chile and bring to a gentle simmer. Remove from the heat, add to a jar with the radishes, and set aside.

Cut the gingerroot into matchsticks. Remove the chard leaves from the stems. Finely chop the stems and shred the leaves. Boil the eggs in a small saucepan of water for 6 minutes, then remove, let cool, and peel. Set aside.

Place a medium saucepan over medium heat. Add the wok oil, garlic, and ginger and fry for a few minutes. Add the chard stems and leaves and fry for 3 minutes. Add the chile oil. Remove from the heat, mix well, then remove half the greens to a plate.

Cook the noodles according to the package directions. Whisk the broth and miso into the pan, then bring to a simmer. Divide the noodles between two bowls, then add the reserved greens and boiled eggs. Ladle in the broth. Serve with the pickled radishes on the side.

• •

STORE/MAKE IT VEGAN
Store any leftover pickled radishes in a sterilized jar in the refrigerator for up to three months.

Traditionally, a ham hock is cooked and then the stock is used to make the soup, but I have used a good-quality chicken stock for speed.

Pea & ham soup

with crème fraîche & sourdough croutons

PREP TIME: 10 minutes   COOK TIME: 25 minutes   SERVES: 2

• •

3 tablespoons butter
1 leek, sliced
2 potatoes, peeled and chopped
   into small cubes
scant 3 cups (700ml) chicken stock
2½ cups (400g) fresh or
   frozen peas
1 small handful of mint leaves

3½ ounces (100g) smoked
   ham, sliced
1 handful of Sourdough Croutons
(page 179)
1 tablespoon crème fraîche
olive oil, for drizzling (optional)

Add the butter to a medium saucepan and place over medium heat. Add the leek and potatoes and fry for 6 minutes, or until soft and a little jammy. Pour in the stock and bring to a simmer for 15 minutes, or until the potatoes are soft.

Add the peas and mint and cook for another 2 minutes. Using a stick blender, blend the soup until smooth, then add the ham and heat through.

Ladle into bowls, top with croutons, a dollop of crème fraîche, and a drizzle of olive oil, if desired.

• •

STORE/MAKE IT VEGAN
If you have any leftovers, then store the soup in an airtight container in the refrigerator for up to three days.

• •

Leek & apple soup

with soda bread

PREP TIME: 10 minutes   COOK TIME: 35 minutes   SERVES: 2

• •

3½ ounces (100g)
  smoked pancetta

½ stick (60g) butter

3 leeks, sliced into fine rings

1 green apple, peeled, cored, and
  cut into 1¼-inch (3cm) pieces

1 handful of small
  potatoes, halved

zest and juice of 1 lemon

1 teaspoon fennel seeds

1 teaspoon hot pepper flakes

1¾ cups (400ml) cider

7 ounces (200g) spring greens,
  finely shredded

1¼ cups (300ml) beef stock

Soda Bread (page 188)

Place a large saucepan over medium heat. Add the pancetta and fry until golden brown and crisp. Remove from the pan and set aside.

Add the butter, leeks, apple, potatoes, and lemon zest and juice to the pan and fry for 15 minutes, stirring frequently.

Add the fennel seeds and hot pepper flakes and fry for 2 minutes, or until aromatic, then add the cider and let the alcohol evaporate for 5 minutes. Add the greens and stock and simmer for another 10 minutes.

Return the pancetta to the pan, stir, and serve with soda bread.

• •

123

STORE/MAKE IT VEGAN
Keep any leftover soup in an airtight container in the refrigerator for up to three days.

What's not to love about this, buttery, garlicky broth with perfectly cooked clams? Serve with bread for dunking and a bowl for the shells.

Arugula & clam soup

with parsley

PREP TIME: 10 minutes   COOK TIME: 10 minutes   SERVES: 2

• •

3½ tablespoons butter

3½ tablespoons olive oil

3 garlic cloves, sliced

4 banana shallots, sliced
  into rings

1 red chile, diced

2¼ pounds (1kg) fresh
  clams, cleaned

1¼ cups (300ml) dry white wine

1¼ cups (300ml) fish stock

zest and juice of 1 lemon

3⅓ cups (100g) arugula

1 large handful of
  parsley, chopped

salt and ground black pepper

Add the butter and olive oil to a large saucepan and place over high heat. Add the garlic, shallots, and red chile and fry until lightly golden.

Tip in the clams, add the wine and stock, cover with a lid, and cook for 3 minutes. Uncover and keep cooking for 2 minutes, or until the soup has reduced a little.

Add the lemon zest and juice, the arugula and parsley. Season to taste with salt and pepper. Serve at once.

• •

STORE/MAKE IT VEGAN
Keep any leftover soup in an airtight container in the refrigerator for up to three days. Reheat it until piping hot before serving.

• •

Brussels sprouts have had a bad rap for some time, but if you don't overcook them, then they are utterly delicious.

Brussels sprouts soup

with cheddar cheese

PREP TIME: 10 minutes   COOK TIME: 25 minutes   SERVES: 2

• •

3 tablespoons olive oil

3 garlic cloves, sliced

2 leeks, sliced

1¼ pounds (600g) Brussels
   sprouts, halved lengthwise

1 tablespoon white wine vinegar

2½ cups (600ml) chicken stock

scant ½ cup (100ml) light cream,
   plus extra for drizzling (optional)

¾ cup (70g) grated
   cheddar cheese

Preheat the oven to 425°F (220°C).

Add the olive oil, garlic, leeks, Brussels sprouts, and vinegar to a large baking pan and roast in the oven for 20 minutes, tossing halfway through.

Tip half the roasted vegetables into a medium saucepan, add the stock, cream, and most of the cheese and bring to a simmer. Using a stick blender, blend until smooth, then top with the remaining vegetables, a little extra cheese, and a drizzle of cream, if desired.

• •

STORE/MAKE IT VEGAN
For a vegan option, swap the chicken stock for vegetable and use vegan cream and vegan cheese instead of the dairy versions.

• •

Ribollita is a brilliant recipe to master as you can make it with what's in season at the time. Here, I used celery root, parsnip, and squash.

Ribollita

with sourdough bread

PREP TIME: 20 minutes   COOK TIME: 1 hour 10 minutes   SERVES: 2

• •

10½ ounces (300g) root vegetables of choice, such as celery root, parsnip, and squash

1 potato

olive oil, for cooking and drizzling

1 onion, finely chopped

3 garlic cloves, finely chopped

2 celery stalks, chopped

a few rosemary sprigs, chopped

14-ounce (400g) can plum tomatoes

½ teaspoon dried red chile

1 whole Parmesan rind plus a little grated Parmesan

21 ounces (600g) jarred white beans

7 ounces (200g) Tuscan kale, coarsely chopped

scant 3 cups (700ml) hot chicken stock

zest and juice of 1 lime

2 slices sourdough bread

salt and ground black pepper

Peel all the root vegetables and the potato into ¾-inch (2cm) pieces and set aside.

Heat 2 tablespoons of olive oil in a Dutch oven over medium heat. Add the onion, garlic, celery, and rosemary and fry for 15 to 20 minutes until soft and sweet.

Add the tomatoes, dried chile, root vegetables, potato, and Parmesan rind and cook over medium to low heat, stirring occasionally, for 15 minutes.

Add the beans, including the liquid they are stored in, the kale, stock, and lemon zest and juice. Bring to a gentle simmer and cook for 30 minutes.

Turn off the heat and lay the slices of bread on top of the soup like a lid. Generously drizzle with olive oil and let stand for 10 minutes.

Season the soup to taste and serve with a good drizzle of olive oil and a dusting of Parmesan, if desired.

• •

STORE/MAKE IT VEGAN
To make this soup vegan, simply leave out the Parmesan rind and use vegetable stock instead of chicken.

This is a take on a Korean kimchi stew. Traditionally, this would contain meat, but I like to make it with extra cabbage and a good broth.

Korean kimchi soup

with tofu & toasted seeds

PREP TIME: 10 minutes   COOK TIME: 20 minutes   SERVES: 2

• •

14-ounce (400g) jar kimchi

7 ounces (200g) cabbage

¾ cup (200g) soft or silken tofu

1 tablespoon gochujang paste

1 tablespoon gochugaru (Korean red pepper powder)

1 tablespoon soy sauce

1 teaspoon granulated sugar

1 tablespoon peanut oil

2 onions, sliced

3 garlic cloves, minced

2½ cups (600ml) Dashi Broth (page 176)

1 teaspoon toasted sesame oil

2 scallions, finely sliced

1 teaspoon toasted sesame seeds

Drain the kimchi through a strainer into a bowl, setting the juice aside, and chopping the kimchi into bite-size pieces. Shred the cabbage and slice the tofu into pieces ½-inch (1cm) thick.

Add the gochujang paste, gochugaru, soy sauce, and sugar to a large bowl. Mix well, then add the kimchi juice. Set aside.

Place a large saucepan over medium heat. Add the peanut oil and onions and fry for 5 minutes, or until golden. Add the garlic and shredded cabbage and fry for another 5 minutes, stirring constantly.

Add the kimchi, the spicy paste, and the broth and bring to a gentle simmer for 5 minutes. Add the tofu, drizzle with the sesame oil, then cover with a lid and simmer for another 5 minutes.

Top with the sliced scallions and toasted sesame seeds before serving.

• •

STORE/MAKE IT VEGAN
To make this soup vegan, use a good-quality mushroom broth instead of the dashi broth.

• •

Tuscan kale

In winter, kale has thicker, curlier, and larger leaves, so is suited to heartier soups. Shredding it finely and then massaging it in oil with your hands makes it tender.

parsley

Fresh parsley has an herbal taste so adding it to soups gives them a greater depth of flavor.

pumpkin

Pumpkins and squashes have a sweet flavor and pair well with strong spices. Try the Winter Squash Soup on page 137.

onions

Onions are available all year round. In winter use them in hearty, warming soups, such as the Beef & Ale Soup on page 139.

mushrooms

Mushrooms excel in the fall and winter. They have an earthy and meaty flavor and go well with onions, garlic, nuts, and greens.

leeks

Leeks have a mild, sweet flavor, which goes well with potatoes, especially in the Leek & Potato Soup on page 135.

celery

Celery has a strong but mild flavor and pairs well with other vegetables, including kale and leeks.

sweet potatoes

Sweet potatoes are one of the most versatile vegetables during late fall and winter. They pair well with carrots, ginger, and mushrooms.

broccoli

You can use both the florets and stems in soup, which can help to reduce food waste.

radishes

Ranging from mild to hot and peppery to pungent, there are lots of varieties of radish to choose from in the fall and winter.

carrots

As carrots have a sweet flavor they partner well with ginger and other spices to make warming winter soups.

squash

From butternut to acorn squash, there are many varieties available. Their earthy and nutty taste pairs well with mushrooms, Brussels sprouts, and apples.

Winter

sage

Sage has an earthy and pungent flavor, which can add depth to soups. Try the Creamy Celery Root Soup on page 157.

purple sprouting broccoli

Purple sprouting broccoli, or winter sprouting broccoli, can cope with big flavors. As it cooks quickly it is suited to jar soups (see page 147).

celery root

Celery root has a sweet, nutty, and mild celery flavor and is perfect for making into soup. Try the recipe on page 157.

potatoes

Potatoes are very versatile in soups and pair well with lots of different foods that we associate with winter, such as leeks and pumpkin.

scallions

Scallions are sweeter and milder than regular onions and go well with leeks, peas, and squash.

avocado

Avocado has a sweet, nutty flavor and when used in wintery soups, gives them a delicate creamy texture.

133

Leek & potato soup

with a rye-baked crouton crumb

PREP TIME: 10 minutes   COOK TIME: 30 minutes   SERVES: 2

• •

3½ tablespoons unsalted butter

1 tablespoon olive oil

4 leeks, sliced into thin rings

1 small handful of thyme leaves

juice of ½ lemon

¾ pound (350g) potatoes,
   peeled and chopped into
   1¼-inch (3cm) chunks

1¾ cups (400ml) chicken stock

scant 1 cup (200ml) heavy cream

3 tablespoons Rye-Baked
   Crouton Crumb (page 179)

Add the butter and olive oil to a medium saucepan and place over medium heat. Add the leeks, thyme, and lemon juice and cook for 15 minutes, stirring frequently until deeply reduced and soft. Scoop out 2 tablespoons and set aside.

Pour in the stock, then add the potatoes. Bring to a boil, then reduce to a simmer and cook for 15 minutes, or until the potatoes are soft to poke with a tip of a knife.

Pour in the cream, then season to taste with salt and pepper. Remove from the heat and, using a stick blender, blend until smooth.

Serve the soup topped with the reserved fried leeks and a sprinkling of the rye crouton crumb.

• •

STORE/MAKE IT VEGAN
If you have any leftover soup, transfer to an airtight container and store in the refrigerator for up to three days.

• •

Winter squash soup

with crispy onions & toasted cashews

PREP TIME: 15 minutes   COOK TIME: 30 minutes   SERVES: 2

1¼ pounds (600g)
   butternut squash

2 tablespoons peanut oil

3 shallots, sliced

3 garlic cloves, diced

2 tablespoons Thai red
   curry paste

6 makrut lime leaves

1¾ cups (400ml) chicken stock

14-ounce (400ml) can
   coconut milk

1 tablespoon fish sauce

1 red chile, sliced

1 handful of Thai basil leaves

½ cup (50g) toasted cashews

1 batch Crispy Onions (page 178)

Peel, seed, and cut the squash into 1¼-inch (3cm) chunks.

Add the oil to a medium saucepan, add the shallots, and fry for 10 minutes, stirring frequently. Add the garlic and fry for another 5 minutes. Add the curry paste and fry for a few minutes, stirring constantly, until fragrant. Add the squash, lime leaves, and stock and simmer for 2 minutes. Add the coconut milk and fish sauce and simmer for another 10 minutes, or until the squash is cooked.

Remove the pan from the heat and, using a stick blender, blend until smooth.

Ladle into bowls and top with red chile, basil, cashews, and crispy onions.

STORE/MAKE IT VEGAN
For a vegan option, use vegan fish sauce and swap the chicken stock for vegetable.

This classic soup gets better with time so feel free to make it a day ahead. Serve with warm Soda Bread (page 189) and plenty of mustard.

Beef & ale soup

with celery root & mustard

PREP TIME: 20 minutes   COOK TIME: 2½ hours   SERVES: 2

• •

1 pound 2 ounces (500g)
   beef brisket

2 onions

2 carrots

2 celery stalks

10½ ounces (300g) celery root

3 garlic cloves

3½ tablespoons light olive oil

3 bay leaves

1 small bunch of thyme

1¼ cups (300ml) Belgian ale

1¾ cups (400ml) beef stock

2 tablespoons tomato paste

2 tablespoons Dijon mustard

salt and ground black pepper

Cut the beef into 2-inch (5cm) chunks, then chop the onions, carrots, and celery stalks. Peel the celery root and cut into cubes. Slice the garlic.

Heat the oil in a large, heavy saucepan and place over medium heat. Generously season the beef with salt and pepper and fry on all sides until golden brown.

Remove the beef to a plate, then add the onions, carrot, celery, celery root, garlic, bay leaves, and thyme to the pan and fry for 10 minutes, stirring frequently.

Add the beef back to the pan, pour in the ale, and stir well, making sure to scrape any bits off the bottom of the pan.

Pour in the stock, add the tomato paste and Dijon mustard, and mix well. Bring to a boil, then reduce the heat and simmer for 2 hours, stirring occasionally.

Once the beef is tender, ladle into bowls, and serve.

• •

STORE/MAKE IT VEGAN
Keep any leftovers in an airtight container in the refrigerator for up to three days.
Make sure it's reheated until piping hot before eating.

• •

This sweet, salty, spicy broth is a must-try. If you have any spicy oil in the refrigerator, then drizzle a little on top before serving.

Satay squash soup

with pickled radishes & crispy onions

PREP TIME: 10 minutes   COOK TIME: 40 minutes   SERVES: 2

• •

10½ ounces (300g) winter squash

1 tablespoon coconut oil

juice of 2 limes

1 tablespoon fish sauce

3 garlic cloves, peeled

3 small shallots, peeled

2½-inch (6cm) piece
   gingerroot, chopped

2 lemongrass stalks, chopped

2 tablespoons sambal oelek

2 tablespoons peanut oil

3 tablespoons peanut butter

1 tablespoon tamarind paste

1 tablespoon soft brown sugar

14-ounce (400ml) can
   coconut milk

8 radishes, thinly sliced

scant ½ cup (100ml) white
   wine vinegar

1 tablespoon superfine sugar

1 teaspoon salt

1 handful of Thai basil

3 tablespoons Crispy Onions
   (page 178)

Peel, seed, and cut the squash into 1¼-inch (3cm) chunks. Preheat the oven to 400°F (200°C).

Add the coconut oil and squash to a high-sided roasting pan. Add half the lime juice and mix well. Season with fish sauce and roast for 20 minutes, tossing halfway.

Add the garlic, shallots, ginger, lemongrass, sambal oelek, oil, and remaining lime juice to a blender and blitz until thick. Blitz in the peanut butter, then tip the mix into a medium saucepan and cook over low heat, stirring frequently, for 15 minutes.

Add the squash to the blender and blitz until smooth, then add it to the pan with the tamarind paste, brown sugar, and coconut milk. Pour in scant 1 cup (200ml) water. Mix well, then taste and season with fish sauce if needed. Simmer for 5 minutes.

Place the radishes in a small bowl with the vinegar, superfine sugar, salt, and scant ½ cup (100ml) cold water and mix. Serve the soup with the radishes, basil, and onions.

• •

STORE/MAKE IT VEGAN
For a vegan option, either use a vegan fish sauce or tamari or soy sauce instead.

I like to use an Italian fennel sausage in this soup, but your favorite vegetarian sausage will work too.

Sausage & bean soup

with hazelnuts & sage

PREP TIME: 10 minutes   COOK TIME: 45 minutes   SERVES: 2

• •

1 tablespoon olive oil

1 onion, sliced

3 garlic cloves, sliced

6 sage leaves, sliced

4 pork and fennel sausages

3½ ounces (100g) winter squash,
   cut into 1¼-inch (3cm) chunks

1 teaspoon fennel seeds

½ teaspoon hot pepper flakes

14-ounce (400g) can
   cannellini beans

1¼ cups (300ml) white wine

1¼ cups (300ml) chicken stock

2 handfuls of Tuscan kale

salt and ground black pepper

Add the olive oil to a large, heavy Dutch oven and place over medium heat. Add the onions and fry for 10 minutes. Add the garlic and sage and fry for another 5 minutes.

Add the sausages and fry for 8 minutes, or until browned. Add the squash, fennel seeds, and hot pepper flakes and fry for a minute. Add the cannellini beans, white wine, and stock and simmer for 20 minutes.

For the last 5 minutes of cooking, add the kale to the pan, then cover with a lid and cook until the kale has wilted. Stir well, then season to taste with salt and pepper and serve.

• •

STORE/MAKE IT VEGAN
To make this soup vegan, use good-quality vegan sausages and vegetable stock instead of chicken.

• •

This sweet potato soup is an explosion of flavors, but if you don't like too much heat, just add half the chile instead.

Sweet potato soup

with peanuts, cilantro & lime

PREP TIME: 10 minutes   COOK TIME: 45 minutes   SERVES: 2

• •

10½ ounces (300g)
   sweet potatoes
2 tablespoons neutral oil
2 red onions, 1 sliced and
   1 coarsely chopped
2½-inch (6cm) piece gingerroot,
   peeled and coarsely chopped
3 garlic cloves, peeled

1 scotch bonnet chile
¼ cup (60g) tomato paste
⅔ cup (150g) crunchy
   peanut butter
2 teaspoons coriander seeds
2 teaspoons ground cumin
½ teaspoon ground cinnamon

14-ounce (400ml) can
   coconut milk
1¾ cups (400ml) vegetable stock
7 ounces (200g) okra, halved
cilantro and lime wedges,
   for serving

Cut the sweet potatoes into ½-inch (1cm) chunks.

Add the oil to a medium saucepan and place over medium heat. Add the sliced onion and fry for 10 minutes, or until soft.

Meanwhile, add the chopped onion, ginger, garlic, chile, tomato paste, and peanut butter to a food processor and blend until smooth.

Add the spices to the onion in the pan and fry for a moment until toasted. Add the peanut paste, reduce the heat to low, and fry for another 10 minutes, stirring frequently. Pour in the coconut milk and stock, then add the sweet potato, cover with a lid, and simmer for 15 minutes, or until the sweet potato is cooked.

Add the okra and stir through. Simmer for another 10 minutes, then season to taste with salt. Serve with cilantro and lime wedges.

• •

STORE/MAKE IT VEGAN
If you have any leftover soup, transfer to an airtight container and store in the refrigerator for up to three days.

• •

Glass noodles cook in no time at all, and with a few ingredients you can pack in all the flavors you want on a chilly winter's day.

Winter in a jar

Mushroom, glass noodle, smoked tofu & broccoli soup

PREP TIME: 10 minutes   COOK TIME: 4 minutes   SERVES: 2

• •

2 tablespoons sambal oelek

2 teaspoons sesame oil

2 teaspoons smooth
   peanut butter

2 teaspoons fish sauce

3½ ounces (100g) glass noodles
   or vermicelli

7 ounces (200g) mixed
   mushrooms, chopped

3½ ounces (100g) smoked tofu,
   cut into ½-inch (1cm) chunks

4 heads of purple sprouting
   broccoli, finely chopped

1 red chile, sliced

Add the sambal oelek and sesame oil to two 25-ounce (750ml) mason jars followed by the peanut butter and fish sauce. Top with the rice noodles, mushrooms, tofu, broccoli, and chile, then pop the lid on.

When ready to eat, pour in 1¾ cups (400ml) boiling water and let stand for 4 minutes. Mix well and eat at once.

• •

STORE/MAKE IT VEGAN
Put the second jar in the refrigerator for lunch for later in the week.

• •

I always use good-quality jarred beans as these are cooked in a flavorsome stock, but you can use a can and a scant 1 cup (200ml) stock.

Kale & white bean soup

with Pecorino Romano

PREP TIME: 15 minutes   COOK TIME: 35 minutes   SERVES: 2

• •

scant ½ cup (100ml) olive oil

2 onions, sliced

3 garlic cloves, sliced

2 celery stalks, sliced

8 sage leaves, chopped

generous ¾ cup (100g) sliced
   green olives

1 green chile, sliced

¾ cup (175ml) white wine

zest and juice of 1 lemon

21 ounces (600g) jarred
   haricot or cannellini beans

2 large handfuls of kale

scant 1 cup (200ml) chicken stock

½ cup (50g) grated Pecorino
   Romano cheese

Add the olive oil to a medium, heavy saucepan and place over medium heat. Add the onions and cook, stirring frequently, for 15 minutes, or until the onions have really broken down and are a golden color.

Add the garlic, celery, sage leaves, olives, and green chile and fry for 5 minutes. Pour in the wine, then increase the heat and let the alcohol evaporate for 5 minutes. Add the lemon juice and zest, the cannellini beans with their liquid, the kale, and the chicken stock and simmer for 10 minutes.

Ladle the soup into bowls and serve with a good amount of grated cheese.

• •

STORE/MAKE IT VEGAN
To make this soup vegan, use vegetable stock instead of chicken and swap the cheese for a vegan one or just leave it out.

• •

My Scottish granny always made this soup with a whole chicken, but I'm using thighs to make it faster. Be sure to use a good-quality stock.

Cock-a-leekie soup

with rice & dried prunes

PREP TIME: 15 minutes   COOK TIME: 40 minutes   SERVES: 2

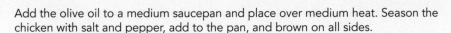

1 tablespoon light olive oil

4 skinless chicken thighs, bone in, about 5 ounces (140g) each

generous 2 cups (500ml) chicken stock

3 bay leaves

2 leeks, halved lengthwise, thinly shredded

1 carrot, sliced into half-moons

1 celery stalk, coarsely chopped

¼ cup (50g) long-grain rice

8 dried prunes, coarsely chopped

salt and ground black pepper

lemon wedges, for serving (optional)

Add the olive oil to a medium saucepan and place over medium heat. Season the chicken with salt and pepper, add to the pan, and brown on all sides.

Add the stock and bay leaves to the pan and simmer for 5 minutes. Add the leeks, carrots, and celery and simmer for another 10 minutes. Next, add the rice and prunes and simmer for another 15 minutes, or until the rice is cooked.

Remove the chicken from the pan and shred the meat, discarding the bones. Add the shredded chicken back to the soup. Serve with lemon wedges, if desired.

STORE/MAKE IT VEGAN
Keep any leftover soup in an airtight container in the refrigerator for up to three days, or freeze for up to three months.

Soup for a crowd

Mexican bean soup

with kale & chicken

This black bean soup is inspired by a soup I ate in Tulum in Mexico. Even though the soup is served with a perfectly cooked roast chicken, the soup is the hero here. It's ideal for a crowd as the shredded roast chicken goes a long way. If you have nonmeat-eaters in the group, the soup on its own with the toppings is also perfect.

SERVING A CROWD: Mexican bean soup

Serve the roasted chicken on the table with the black bean soup and any toppings you fancy, such as avocado, cheese, cilantro, and chile. Perfect with a Mexican beer.

PREP TIME: 15 minutes   COOK TIME: 50 minutes   SERVES: 6 to 8

4½-pound (2kg) chicken

¼ cup (60ml) olive oil

3 tablespoons chipotle paste

1 tablespoon cumin seeds

juice of 2 limes, plus 1 in wedges

2 large onions, diced

5 large tomatoes, chopped

8 garlic cloves, chopped

1 tablespoon dried oregano

1 bunch of thyme, leaves removed

1 teaspoon ground cumin

1 teaspoon ground coriander

2 teaspoons hot pepper flakes

2 x 14-ounce (400g) cans black
  beans, drained and rinsed

8 cups (2L) chicken stock

1 bunch of kale, finely shredded

2 avocados, peeled and diced

5½ ounces (150g) queso fresco

1 bunch of cilantro

1 jalapeño chile, sliced

salt

Ask your butcher to spatchcock the chicken.

Preheat the oven to 400°F (200°C).

Add 1 tablespoon of olive oil to a large bowl, add the chipotle paste, cumin seeds, and half the lime juice. Mix well, then smother it all over the chicken. Season with salt and roast for 50 minutes.

Meanwhile, place a large, heavy saucepan over high heat and add the remaining oil. Add the onions, tomatoes, and garlic and fry for 5 minutes. Reduce the heat to medium, add the herbs and remaining spices, then stir and cook for another 4 minutes. Add the beans and stock. Stir, then cover and cook for 40 minutes.

Add the remaining lime juice and season with more salt, if needed. Using a stick blender, blend a third of the soup. Add the kale, then reduce the heat to low, and simmer, stirring occasionally.

Once the chicken is cooked, pour the chicken juices into the soup and slice the chicken. Transfer to a plate and serve.

This velvety soup is simple to make. Celery root is an understated vegetable, but once you've tried it like this you will never look back.

Creamy celery root soup

with chestnuts & crispy sage

PREP TIME: 15 minutes   COOK TIME: 25 minutes   SERVES: 2

• •

2 tablespoons olive oil

1 leek, sliced

1 celery stalk, diced

9 ounces (250g) celery root, peeled and chopped

½ teaspoon hot pepper flakes

1¾ cups (400ml) vegetable stock

3½ tablespoons butter

½ bunch of sage leaves

½ cup (100g) cooked chestnuts

6 tablespoons heavy cream

Add the olive oil to a medium saucepan and place over medium heat. Add the leek and fry for 10 minutes, or until soft. Add the celery and celery root and fry for another 5 minutes. Add the hot pepper flakes and stock and simmer for 10 minutes.

Meanwhile, add the butter to a large skillet over medium heat. Add the sage leaves and fry until crisp. Remove from the pan with a slotted spoon and set aside, then add the chestnuts to the skillet and cook for 5 minutes, or until a little crisp and golden and the butter is a dark brown. Remove from the heat.

Add the cream to the soup with half the sage leaves and chestnuts. Remove from the heat and, using a stick blender, blend until smooth.

Ladle the soup into bowls and top with the remaining sage and chestnuts and a drizzle of the brown butter.

• •

STORE/MAKE IT VEGAN
Store any leftover soup in an airtight container in the refrigerator for up to three days.

Serve this warming soup with lime wedges, a dollop of crème fraîche, some sliced jalapeño chiles, and grated cheese.

Tex-Mex chili

with roasted sweet potato

PREP TIME: 15 minutes   COOK TIME: 45 minutes   SERVES: 2

• •

2 tablespoons olive oil

1 large sweet potato, diced

2 onions, diced

4 garlic cloves, sliced

2 teaspoons sweet
   smoked paprika

1 tablespoon ground cumin

1 tablespoon ground coriander

1 teaspoon ground cinnamon

10½ ounces (300g) lean
   ground beef

1 tablespoon dried oregano

14-ounce (400g) can kidney
   beans, drained and rinsed

14-ounce (400g) can
   chopped tomatoes

8 pickled jalapeño
   chiles, chopped

3½ ounces (100g) smoked jarred
   red peppers, chopped

1¼ cups (300ml) beef stock

salt and ground black pepper

Preheat the oven to 400°F (200°C). Add a tablespoon of oil to a small baking pan and toss in the sweet potato. Season well with salt and pepper and roast in the oven for 20 minutes.

Meanwhile, add the remaining oil to a medium saucepan and place over medium heat. Add the onions and fry for 5 minutes. Add the garlic and fry for another 2 minutes. Add the spices and toast for a minute, or until fragrant. Add the ground beef and fry, breaking the beef up with a wooden spoon and making sure it's evenly mixed for 10 minutes.

Add the dried oregano, beans, chopped tomatoes, jalapeños, jarred peppers, and stock and simmer for 15 minutes. Once the sweet potato is roasted, add it to the soup. You want this to blip away and reduce slightly but still remain soupy, so feel free to add extra stock, if needed. Serve with any toppings you like.

• •

STORE/MAKE IT VEGAN
Store any leftover soup in an airtight container in the refrigerator for up to three days.

• •

I love to make this ramen when I feel I need a nourishing soup. Make sure you have all your prep ready, as this comes together quickly.

Broccoli & leek ramen

with kale & boiled eggs

PREP TIME: 15 minutes   COOK TIME: 25 minutes   SERVES: 2

• •

2 tablespoons sesame oil

1 small head of broccoli, sliced into thin florets

2 handfuls of kale, finely shredded

1 tablespoon sesame seeds

1 leek, thinly sliced

1¼-inch (3cm) piece gingerroot, peeled and julienned

3 garlic cloves, sliced

2½ cups (600ml) Dashi Broth (page 176)

7 ounces (200g) ramen noodles

2 tablespoons pickled ginger

1 red chile, diced

2 soft-boiled eggs, halved

salt

Preheat the oven to 425°F (220°C).

Drizzle ½ tablespoon of oil over the broccoli and arrange on one side of a large baking sheet. Place the kale in a bowl, season with salt, and drizzle with ½ tablespoon of oil. Toss well and arrange on the other side of the baking sheet. Sprinkle over the sesame seeds and roast in the oven for 10 minutes.

Add the remaining oil to a medium saucepan and place over high heat. Add the leek and fry for 10 minutes, or until golden. Add the ginger and garlic and fry for a moment. Pour in the broth and let simmer.

Meanwhile, cook the noodles according to the package directions, then drain and rinse under cold water. Arrange the noodles in two ramen bowls. Remove the greens from the oven and mix well, then return to the oven for 5 minutes, or until the kale is crispy and the broccoli is golden. Ladle the stock into the bowls and top with a pile of crispy kale, broccoli, pickled ginger, chile, and eggs.

• •

STORE/MAKE IT VEGAN
For a vegan option, use just kombu in the broth or use a good-quality vegetable stock and omit the boiled eggs.

This hearty, well-balanced soup is a true Mediterranean combination. The key is to buy good-quality chorizo for this recipe.

Kale & chorizo soup

with spelt & parsley

PREP TIME: 10 minutes   COOK TIME: 30 minutes   SERVES: 2

• •

1 tablespoon olive oil

7 ounces (200g) raw
  chorizo, diced

2 onions, sliced

3 garlic cloves, sliced

1 tablespoon sweet
  smoked paprika

14-ounce (400g) can
  chopped tomatoes

generous 2 cups (500ml)
  chicken stock

⅔ cup (100g) spelt grains

juice of 1 lemon

5½ ounces (150g) kale, shredded

1 bunch of parsley, chopped

Add the olive oil to a medium saucepan and place over medium heat. Add the diced chorizo and fry for 5 minutes, or until the oil has been released and the chorizo has taken on a bit of color.

Scoop the chorizo out with a slotted spoon and set aside on a plate, then add the onion and garlic to the pan and fry for 5 minutes. Add the paprika, tomatoes, and stock and bring to a boil. Tip in the spelt grains and fried chorizo, cover with a lid, and simmer for 15 minutes.

Uncover and add the lemon juice and kale. Cook for another 5 minutes, or until the kale is wilted. Stir half the parsley through the soup, then divide the soup between bowls and top with the remaining parsley.

• •

STORE/MAKE IT VEGAN
Make sure the soup is cold before transferring it to an airtight container and storing it in the refrigerator for two days.

• •

Toasting the orzo gives this soup a lovely nutty taste. I like to serve this with some extra grated Parmesan.

Lemony chicken soup

with orzo & Tuscan kale

PREP TIME: 10 minutes   COOK TIME: 30 minutes   SERVES: 2

• •

1 tablespoon olive oil

1 cup (100g) orzo

2 skinless, boneless chicken
   breasts, 7 ounces (200g) each

juice of 2 lemons and zest of 1

4 garlic cloves, 4 chopped
   and 1 left whole

generous 2 cups (500ml)
   chicken stock

generous ¾ cup (60g) grated
   Parmesan and rind

⅓ cup (50g) toasted pine nuts

1 red chile

3½ ounces (100g) Tuscan kale

salt and ground black pepper

Add the olive oil to a medium saucepan and place over medium heat. Add the orzo and toast it for 5 minutes, or until lightly browned. Remove the orzo and set aside.

Add the chicken to the pan and sear on all sides until golden. Add the juice of one lemon and the zest, then add the chopped garlic and fry for 2 minutes. Pour in the stock, add the Parmesan rind, and bring to a simmer. Add the orzo and cook for 10 minutes.

Meanwhile, add the grated Parmesan, pine nuts, the whole garlic clove, red chile, the remaining lemon juice, and the kale to a blender or food processor and blend until a smooth sauce has formed.

Remove the chicken from the pan and shred the meat. Remove the Parmesan rind and discard, then stir the sauce through the soup. Season to taste with salt and pepper and stir the chicken back through. Ladle into bowls and serve.

• •

STORE/MAKE IT VEGAN

Keep any leftovers in an airtight container in the refrigerator for up to three days.

• •

This buttermilk broccoli soup feels quite decadent but really isn't. I like to serve with a drizzle of chile oil, but any good-quality oil works too.

Broccoli soup

with chile oil & garlic & lemon toasts

PREP TIME: 15 minutes   COOK TIME: 20 minutes   SERVES: 2

• •

3 tablespoons olive oil

1 pound (450g) broccoli, woody
  stems trimmed

4 garlic cloves, sliced

1 red chile, sliced

1 leek, sliced

1 large potato, peeled and
  cut into 1¼-inch (3cm) chunks

generous 2 cups (500ml)
  vegetable stock

scant 1 cup (200ml) buttermilk

salt and ground black pepper

Chile Oil (page 200), for drizzling

Garlic & Lemon Toasts
  (page 190), for serving

Preheat the oven to 425°F (220°C).

Add half of the olive oil to a sheet pan and toss in the broccoli, garlic, and chile and mix well. Roast in the oven for 15 minutes, or until slightly crisp and cooked.

Meanwhile, add the remaining olive oil to a medium saucepan and place over high heat. Add the leek and fry for 5 minutes, then add the potato and stock and simmer for 15 minutes.

Once the broccoli is ready, add most of it to the soup, setting aside a little for the top. Pour the buttermilk into the pan, then remove from the heat and, using a stick blender, blend until smooth. Season to taste with salt and pepper.

Ladle the soup into bowls, top with the reserved broccoli, then drizzle with the chile oil. Serve with garlic and lemon toasts.

• •

STORE/MAKE IT VEGAN
Keep any leftover soup in an airtight container in the refrigerator for up to three days.

• •

Using miso gives this soup a delicious hit of umami. I like to serve it with my Chopped Herb Oil (page 201).

Kale & potato soup

with leeks & chopped herb oil

PREP TIME: 15 minutes   COOK TIME: 35 minutes   SERVES: 2

• •

2 tablespoons olive oil

2 leeks, sliced

4 garlic cloves, chopped

2 celery stalks, diced

juice of 1 lemon

7 ounces (200g) small new
   potatoes, quartered

scant 3 cups (700ml) chicken stock

7 ounces (200g) Tuscan kale,
   inner stems removed and
   leaves shredded

2 tablespoons miso

salt

2 tablespoons Chopped Herb
   Oil (page 201), for serving

Preheat the oven to 400°F (200°C).

Add 1 tablespoon of olive oil to a medium saucepan and place over medium heat. Add the leeks and fry for 10 minutes, or until soft. Add the garlic and celery and fry for another 5 minutes. Add the lemon juice, potatoes, and stock and bring to a boil. Reduce the heat and simmer for 15 minutes.

Meanwhile, place half the kale in a bowl and drizzle over the remaining olive oil. Season generously with salt, then arrange on a large baking sheet and cook in the oven for 10 minutes, tossing halfway through, until the kale is crispy and dark green.

Once the potatoes are cooked, add the remaining raw kale, and cook for another 5 minutes, or until wilted. Add the miso and mix well, making sure the miso is well distributed throughout the soup.

Top the soup with the crispy kale and serve with the herb oil on top.

• •

STORE/MAKE IT VEGAN
For a vegan option, substitute the chicken stock with vegetable.

• •

Extra good stuff!

Bases & stocks

Chicken stock

2 tablespoons peanut oil
4½ pounds (2kg) raw
  chicken bones and carcasses
3 onions, chopped, skins on

4 celery stalks, chopped
1 head of garlic, halved
4 bay leaves
1 teaspoon flaky sea salt

1 tablespoon peppercorns
4 carrots, chopped

Preheat the oven to 400°F (200°C). Add all the ingredients to a large roasting
pan and mix well. Roast for 1 hour, then mix again. Carefully pour in generous
2 cups (500ml) water and roast for another 20 minutes. Remove the pan and
add the contents to a large saucepan. Pour in 6¼ cups (1.5L) water, making
sure to scrape all the crispy bits off the pan into the saucepan. Cover the
saucepan and cook over medium heat for 1 hour. Strain the liquid and use at
once, or once it has cooled, freeze or refrigerate.
PREP: 10 minutes   COOK: 2½ hours   MAKES: 8½ cups (2L)

Roasted vegetable broth

3 tablespoons olive oil
3 onions, skin on, chopped
1 head of garlic, halved skin on
3 carrots, coarsely chopped

2 large tomatoes, halved
5 celery stalks,
coarsely chopped
4 bay leaves

1 small bunch of thyme
1 teaspoon flaky sea salt
1 tablespoon
black peppercorns

Preheat the oven to 400°F (200°C). Add all the ingredients to a large roasting
pan and mix well. Roast for 45 minutes, or until golden. Tip the veg into a
large stockpot. Pour a little water into the roasting pan, making sure you get all
the roasting juices, then pour into the pot and top off with 10 cups (2.5L) cold
water. Bring to a boil, reduce the heat, and simmer for 1 hour. Let cool slightly.
Strain the liquid and use at once, or once it has cooled, freeze or refrigerate.
PREP: 10 minutes   COOK: 1¾ hours   MAKES: 8½ cups (2L)

Fish stock

2 tablespoons butter
2 onions, coarsely chopped
2¼ pounds (1kg) white
  fish bones and heads
2 ripe tomatoes, halved
4 bay leaves
1¾ cups (400ml) white wine
2 heads of fennel, chopped

1 bunch of parsley stems
1 small bunch of thyme
skin of 1 lemon, peeled
  into strips

Add the butter to a large stockpot, then add the chopped onions and fry over high heat until the onions start to brown. Add all the remaining ingredients and 8½ cups (2L) water and bring to a boil. Reduce the heat and simmer for 30 minutes, skimming off any scum that rises to the surface of the stock. Strain the liquid and use at once, or once it has cooled, freeze or refrigerate.
PREP: 10 minutes   COOK: 40 to 45 minutes   MAKES: 8½ cups (2L)

Beef bone broth

4½ pounds (2kg) beef bones, preferably a mix of marrow bones and bones with a little meat on them, such as oxtail, short ribs, etc.	1 head of garlic, halved
	2 leeks, cut into 3-inch (7.5cm) pieces
	4 celery stalks, cut into 2-inch (5cm) pieces
	4 bay leaves
2 carrots, coarsely chopped	2 tablespoons black peppercorns
1 onion, quartered	1 tablespoon cider vinegar

Preheat the oven to 400°F (200°C). Add all the bones to a large roasting pan. Toss in the carrots, onion, garlic, and leeks and roast for 50 minutes tossing halfway through. Fill a large stockpot with 10 cups (2.5L) water and add the remaining ingredients. Scrape the roasted bones and vegetables into the stockpot along with any juices, adding more water if necessary to cover the bones and vegetables. Cover the pot with a lid and bring to a gentle boil. Reduce the heat to low and cook, skimming off any foam and excess fat that rises to the surface, for at least 10 hours. Strain the liquid and use at once, or once it has cooled, freeze or refrigerate.

PREP: 10 minutes   COOK: 11 hours   MAKES: 8½ cups (2L)

Dashi broth

1 ounce (30g) dried kombu
3 ounces (80g) dried
  bonito flakes

Add 8½ cups (2L) water to a stockpot, then add the kombu and place over low heat. Bring to a very gentle simmer, then remove from the heat and add the bonito flakes. Let stand for 10 minutes. Strain through a fine-mesh strainer and use at once or keep in the refrigerator for up to a week.
PREP: 15 minutes   COOK: 20 minutes   MAKES: 8½ cups (2L)

Spiced broth

1 tablespoon flaky salt	4 cardamom pods, bashed	3 onions, quartered
3 tablespoons fish sauce	3 cloves	2 lemongrass stalks
	2 tablespoons coriander seeds	6 garlic cloves, skins on, bashed
	4½ pounds (2kg) meaty	2 red chiles
	beef bones	5 x 2½-inch (6cm) pieces
	2¼ pounds (1kg)	gingerroot, sliced
	marrow bones, halved	12 star anise
	2 tablespoons superfine sugar	3 cinnamon sticks

Place a large stockpot over high heat until smoking hot, then add the onions, lemongrass, garlic, chiles, and gingerroot and char for 5 minutes. Reduce the heat to medium, add the spices, and toast them for a minute. Add the bones, then pour in 14 cups (3.5L) water. Cover with a lid and gently simmer for 4 hours, checking the stock occasionally and skimming off any scum that rises to the top. Strain the broth into another pan, discarding the bones and spices. Season to taste with the sugar, salt, and fish sauce. Use at once, or once it has cooled, refrigerate or freeze.

PREP: 10 minutes   COOK: 4¼ hours   MAKES: 10 cups (2.5L)

Crunchy toppings

Crispy onions

1¼ cups (300ml) vegetable oil
10 banana shallots, sliced into
  half-moons
1 teaspoon flaky sea salt

Line a plate with paper towels and set aside. Heat the oil in a large skillet over medium to low heat. Add the sliced onions and fry, stirring frequently, for 15 minutes, or until all the onions are golden brown. Remove with a large slotted spoon to the lined plate and sprinkle with the salt. Once cooled, the onions will be crispy and delicious. Store in an airtight container for up to a month.
PREP: 10 minutes   COOK: 15 minutes
MAKES: 17-ounce (500ml) mason jar

Crispy rice

1¼ cups (300ml) vegetable or
  sunflower oil

generous 1 cup (200g) cooked
  but cold rice (I use leftover
  rice the next day)
½ teaspoon flaky sea salt

Line a baking sheet with paper towels. Heat the oil in a large, deep saucepan to 350 to 375°F (180 to 190°C). Working in two batches, fry half the rice until it pops and rises to the surface. Remove with a slotted spoon and lay out on the lined baking sheet. Deep-fry the remaining rice and let drain on the baking sheet. Season with salt, then let cool. Once cooled, store it in a sterilized jar.
PREP: 10 minutes   COOK: 10 minutes
MAKES: 1¼-cup (300ml) jar

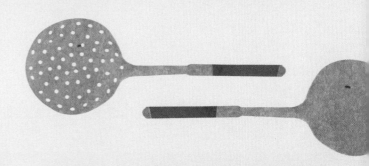

Rye-baked crouton crumb

5½ ounces (150g) rye bread
3 tablespoons olive oil
zest of 1 lemon

1 garlic clove, grated
½ teaspoon flaky sea salt
pinch of hot pepper flakes

Blitz the rye bread in a food processor until it is coarse breadcrumbs. Heat the olive oil in a large skillet over medium heat, add the breadcrumbs, lemon zest, and grated garlic, and fry for 6 minutes, stirring frequently. When the mix becomes toasted and crunchy, add the salt and hot pepper flakes and cook for another minute. Remove from the heat and let chill before storing in an airtight container.
PREP: 2 minutes   COOK: 6 to 8 minutes
MAKES: 7 ounces (200g)

Sourdough croutons

3 thick slices of
  sourdough bread
3 tablespoons olive oil
1 teaspoon flaky sea salt

1 tablespoon red
  wine vinegar

Preheat the oven to 350°F (180°C). Tear the sourdough bread into bite-size pieces and add to a large bowl with the remaining ingredients. Mix well, making sure the bread is coated evenly all over. Arrange the bread on a large baking sheet in a single layer and bake in the oven for 10 to 15 minutes until golden and crisp, tossing halfway through.
PREP: 2 minutes   COOK: 10 to 15 minutes
MAKES: 7 ounces (200g)

Seasonal roasted veg

Spring

1 handful of kale
2 scallions
1 handful of radishes
2 red onions

2 tablespoons olive oil
2 tablespoons red wine vinegar
salt and ground black pepper

Preheat the oven to 400°F (200°C). Peel and chop the vegetables into bite-size pieces. Add all the ingredients to a large baking sheet and mix well. Season with salt and pepper and roast in the oven for 20 minutes, mixing halfway through.
PREP: 10 minutes   COOK: 20 minutes   MAKES: enough for 2

Summer

2 zucchini
1 head of fennel
1 tablespoon thyme leaves
2 tablespoons olive oil

juice of 1 lemon
5½ ounces (150g) Swiss
   chard, chopped
salt and ground black pepper

Preheat the oven to 400°F (200°C). Chop the zucchini and fennel into bite-size pieces, then add to a large baking sheet, with the thyme, olive oil, and lemon juice. Mix well, season with salt and pepper, and roast in the oven for 30 minutes. For the last 5 minutes, toss in the chard and return to the oven for 5 minutes.
PREP: 10 minutes   COOK: 30 minutes   MAKES: enough for 2

Fall

leek	1 handful of sage leaves
red bell peppers	2 tablespoons olive oil
ounces (200g) pumpkin	juice of 1 orange
garlic cloves	salt and ground black pepper

reheat the oven to 400°F (200°C). Peel and chop the vegetables
nto bite-size pieces, discarding the seeds. Add all the ingredients
o a large baking sheet and mix well. Season with salt and pepper
nd roast in the oven for 35 minutes, tossing halfway through.
REP: 10 minutes   COOK: 35 minutes   MAKES: enough for 2

Winter

2 parsnips	2 tablespoons olive oil
1 beet	1 teaspoon dried oregano
1 carrot	1 tablespoon wine vinegar
1 small handful of rosemary	salt and ground black pepper

Preheat the oven to 400°F (200°C). Peel and chop the vegetables
into bite-size pieces. Add all the ingredients to a large baking
sheet and mix well. Season with salt and pepper and roast in the
oven for 35 minutes, tossing halfway through.
PREP: 10 minutes   COOK: 35 minutes   MAKES: enough for 2

Bread & feast add-ons

Classic focaccia

with olives & rosemary

PREP TIME: 4½ hours   COOK TIME: 20 minutes   MAKES: 1 tray

• •

2 teaspoons fine salt

1 tablespoon olive oil

¼-ounce (7g) sachet active
    dry yeast

4 cups (560g) strong bread flour

For the tray and top

5 tablespoons olive oil

scant ⅔ cup (60g) pitted
    green olives

3 rosemary stalks, leaves picked

1 teaspoon flaky sea salt

Pour in generous 1¾ cups (470ml) warm water into a bowl. Add the salt, olive oil, and yeast and whisk until combined. Add the flour and mix. Leave for 30 minutes.

Using wet hands, stretch the dough out in the bowl and fold it over in a circular motion. Do this for 3 minutes. Cover and leave in a warm place for 30 minutes, then stretch and fold the dough every 30 minutes for four times in total. Cover the bowl and let chill overnight.

The next day, remove from the refrigerator and leave for 30 minutes. Add 3 tablespoons oil to a large baking sheet and move it all around, making sure the sheet is covered. Tip the dough into the baking sheet, cover, and let prove for 1 hour. Preheat the oven to 425°F (200°C) fan.

Drizzle the remaining oil over the dough, then poke holes into the dough. Sprinkle with the olives, rosemary, and salt and poke them in. Bake for 20 minutes. Remove and let stand for 10 minutes before eating.

• •

STORE/MAKE IT VEGAN

Store freshly baked focaccia at room temperature for a couple of days.

183

• •

This simple seedy loaf is delicious. Serve with some salted butter and a steaming bowl of any soup you fancy from this book.

Seeded bread

with honey

PREP TIME: 2 hours   COOK TIME: 45 minutes   MAKES: 1

• •

vegetable oil, for oiling

2¾ cups (400g) strong whole wheat bread flour

¾ cup (100g) light spelt flour

¼-ounce (7g) sachet active dry yeast

1 tablespoon runny honey or brown sugar

2 teaspoons fine salt

¾ cup (110g) mixed seeds (I used pumpkin, sunflower, poppy, and flaxseeds)

Lightly oil a 2-pound (900g) loaf pan and set aside. Add both flours to a stand mixer fitted with a dough hook and sprinkle in the yeast.

Pour 1¾ cups (400ml) warm water into a measuring cup, then pour in the honey, add the salt, and mix until well combined. Stir the wet ingredients into the flour and mix on medium speed for 8 minutes, or until the dough is soft and springy to the touch. Cover the bowl with a damp dish towel and let rise in a warm place for 1 hour.

Add most of the seeds to the risen dough and mix in until the seeds are well distributed. Tip the dough out and gently press down, then form the dough into a rough oval shape the same size as the pan and place it in the pan, seam-side down. Let prove for 45 minutes. Preheat the oven to 400°F (200°C).

Spray water on top of the loaf and sprinkle over the remaining seeds. Put ½ mug of water in a pan in the bottom of the oven. Bake the loaf on the middle shelf for 45 minutes, or until golden brown. Cool on a cooling rack for 30 minutes before slicing.

• •

STORE/MAKE IT VEGAN
Store freshly baked bread at room temperature for two or three days.

• •

These flatbreads are great as they are so speedy. Once you master the basics, you can experiment with different flavors.

Speedy yogurt flatbreads

with hot pepper flakes

PREP TIME: 2 minutes   COOK TIME: 8 minutes   MAKES: 4 breads

• •

1½ cups (195g) self-rising flour
1 cup (230g) plain yogurt
1 teaspoon fine sea salt
zest of 1 lemon
pinch of hot pepper flakes
1 tablespoon olive oil
1 tablespoon salted butter

Add all the ingredients, except the butter, to a large bowl, Mix well, then tip it out onto a clean counter and knead until the dough is soft and springy.

Using clean hands, divide the dough into four balls and roll out into 5½-inch (14cm) round breads, about ⅛ inch (3mm) thick.

Place a stovetop grill pan over high heat, and, once smoking hot, fry the breads, two at a time, for about 2 minutes on each side until charred and puffed up. Remove from the pan and repeat with the remaining breads. Once all are done, rub over the butter and serve.

• •

STORE/MAKE IT VEGAN
Store these flatbreads in an airtight container in the refrigerator for up to three days.

• •

Soda bread

served with butter

PREP TIME: 2 minutes   COOK TIME: 30 minutes   MAKES: 1 small loaf

• •

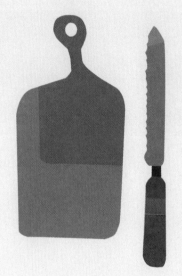

scant 2 cups (250g) all-purpose
   flour, plus extra for dusting
generous 1¾ cups (250g) whole
   wheat flour
1 teaspoon salt
1 teaspoon baking soda
1¾ cups (400ml) buttermilk
butter, for serving

Preheat the oven to 400°F (200°C) and line a baking sheet with baking parchment.

Add both flours, the salt, and baking soda to a large bowl and mix to combine. Make a well in the center and, using a clean hand, mix briefly. Pour in the buttermilk and mix until it all comes together into a dough. There's no need to give it a proper kneading as this is a rough bread.

Tip the dough out onto a lightly floured counter and shape into a ball. Transfer the dough to the lined baking sheet and, using a knife, slash a deep cross in the top. Dust the top with flour.

Bake in the oven for 30 minutes, or until the loaf is golden brown. Transfer to a cooling rack to cool slightly, then eat warm with butter.

• •

STORE/MAKE IT VEGAN
This is best eaten the same day, but store any leftovers at room temperature for a couple of days.

• •

What's not to love about this oily, garlicy, buttery toast? This is quicker than garlic bread, so it's easy to make before serving with soup.

Garlic & lemon toasts

with olive oil

PREP TIME: 2 minutes   COOK TIME: 6 to 8 minutes   SERVES: 2

• •

2 teaspoons olive oil
1 tablespoon butter,
   at room temperature
zest of 1 lemon
1 garlic clove, grated

2 slices of bread of your choice
   (I used sourdough)
½ teaspoon flaky sea salt

Add the olive oil, butter, lemon zest, and grated garlic to a bowl and mix well.

Place a pan that is large enough to fit the toast in over medium heat. Spread half the oil and garlic mix on one side of the bread and place that side down in the pan. Smear the rest on the side facing up and toast for 3 minutes on each side, or until deeply golden and crisp. Remove and repeat with the remaining bread and mixture. Cut into slices, sprinkle with the salt, and serve at once.

• •

STORE/MAKE IT VEGAN
For a vegan option, either use all olive oil instead of butter or use a vegan butter or spread.

This is a good way to get extra fiber into your diet. For those days when you feel hungry and want something more than bread, this is for you.

Bulky mixed grain add-in

with quinoa, spelt & farro

PREP TIME: 2 minutes   COOK TIME: 25 minutes   MAKES: enough for 4 people

• •

1 cup (250ml) vegetable stock
1 tablespoon peanut oil
¼ cup (50g) long-grain rice
generous ½ cup (100g)
   mixed quinoa
⅓ cup (50g) pearled spelt

¼ cup (50g) pearled farro
1 teaspoon salt
zest and juice of 1 lemon

Pour the stock into a medium saucepan and place over high heat until hot.

Add the oil to a large, heavy saucepan, then add the rice and all the grains. Toast over medium heat for a few minutes. Add the hot stock, salt, and lemon zest and juice and bring to a boil. Once boiling, cover with a lid, reduce the heat to low, and simmer for 12 minutes.

Remove the pan from the heat and let stand with the lid on for another 8 minutes. Fluff up all the grains and serve alongside or stirred through a soup of your choice.

• •

STORE/MAKE IT VEGAN
Once cooled, store in an airtight container in the refrigerator for up to a week.

The perfect grilled cheese to dip in any soup

2 tablespoons unsalted butter
2 slices of thick white
   sandwich loaf

⅔ cup (60g) grated cheese or
   mix of cheddar, red Leicester,
   mozzarella, Gruyère, Comte

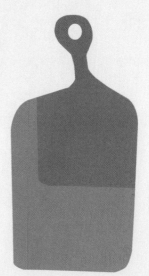

Butter both slices of bread and spread the cheese out on the unbuttered side. Top with the other slice of bread, making sure the buttered sides are both facing outwards. Place a medium pan over medium to low heat, add the toastie, and weigh down with another pan or cast-iron lid. The key to a good toastie is slow and steady. Fry for 6 minutes, then flip over and repeat on the other side, or until each side is perfectly golden and the cheese is oozy. Slice and serve.
PREP: 5 minutes   COOK: 12 minutes   MAKES: 1 sandwich

Simple quesadillas for any spiced soup

1 tablespoon olive oil
2 flour tortillas
⅔ cup (30g) grated
cheddar cheese

¼ cup (30g) grated mozzarella
1 tablespoon chopped
pickled jalapeño chile
1 scallion, finely sliced

Add the olive oil to a large skillet and place over medium heat. Lay one of the
tortillas out on a cutting board and sprinkle over the cheeses, jalapeños, and
scallions. Carefully transfer to the pan and top with the other tortilla. Fry for a
few minutes, or until crisp and golden. Using a spatula, flip the tortilla over and
fry until crisp and golden on the other side. Slide the quesadilla out of the pan
and cut into wedges. Serve at once.
PREP: 5 minutes   COOK: 6 to 8 minutes   MAKES: 8 wedges

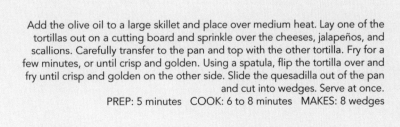

Hearty cornbread

with butter

PREP TIME: 25 minutes   COOK TIME: 20 minutes   SERVES: 6 to 8

• •

3 ears of corn

½ stick (60g) melted butter, plus
   extra for melting and serving

scant 1 cup (120g)
   all-purpose flour

1 cup (160g) yellow cornmeal

3¾ tablespoons (40g) brown sugar

1 teaspoon baking powder

½ teaspoon baking soda

½ teaspoon flaky sea salt

1 teaspoon smoked
   sweet pimento

scant 1 cup (240ml) buttermilk

2 tablespoons runny honey

2 large eggs

1 jalapeño chile, sliced

Preheat the oven to 400°F (200°C).

Husk the corn and slice the kernels from the cob. Set aside. Grease a 9-inch (23cm) cast-iron skillet with butter and place the skillet in the oven to heat up.

Whisk the flour, cornmeal, sugar, baking powder, baking soda, salt, and pimento together in a large bowl until combined. Make a well in the center of the dry ingredients and add the buttermilk, honey, most of the corn, and the eggs. Mix with a wooden spoon, then add the melted butter and mix until combined.

Carefully remove the hot skillet from the oven, pour in the batter, and sprinkle over the jalapeños and reserved corn. Return the pan to the oven and bake for 20 minutes, or until a toothpick comes out clean. Let chill in the refrigerator for 10 minutes, then serve with cold butter.

• •

STORE/MAKE IT VEGAN
Store freshly baked cornbread at room temperature for two days.

Warm and flaky, these are delicious. Try not to overwork the dough as it needs to come together quickly, ensuring everything stays cold.

Classic buttermilk biscuits

with butter & honey

PREP TIME: 5 minutes   COOK TIME: 18 to 20 minutes   MAKES: 8 biscuits

• •

2¾ cups (360g) all-purpose flour, plus extra for dusting

1½ tablespoons baking powder

1 teaspoon fine table salt

1 stick (115g) extra-cold unsalted butter, cubed, plus extra for serving

1¼ cups (300ml) cold buttermilk

2 teaspoons runny honey, plus extra for serving

pinch of flaky sea salt

Preheat the oven to 410°F (210°C) and line an 8-inch (20cm) skillet with baking parchment and set aside.

Add the flour, baking powder, and fine salt to a food processor and pulse to combine. Add the butter and pulse until it is coarse breadcrumbs. Pulse in generous 1 cup (270ml) of the buttermilk and the honey until the mixture just comes together.

Tip the dough out onto a lightly floured counter and, using floured hands, flatten into a rectangle ¾-inch (2cm) thick. Fold one side into the center, then the other side on top. Turn the dough horizontally. Gently pat it into a rectangle ¾-inch (2cm) thick again and repeat the folding. Turn the dough horizontally one more time. Gently flatten into a rectangle ¾-inch (2cm) thick. Using a 3-inch (7.5cm) circle biscuit cutter, stamp out eight biscuits. Arrange them in the lined skillet touching each other. Brush the tops with the remaining buttermilk and sprinkle with the sea salt. Bake for 18 to 20 minutes until the tops are golden brown. Remove and let cool for 5 minutes before serving warm with extra butter and a little honey.

• •

STORE/MAKE IT VEGAN
Store any leftovers in an airtight container at room temperature for up to five days.

• •

Oils & aioli

Chile oil

12 dried guindilla Italian chiles,
  lightly crushed
1¾ cups (400ml) good-quality
  olive oil

Add the chiles to a medium saucepan and pour in the oil. Place over medium heat and bring to a bubble. This should take about 6 minutes. Remove from the heat and let cool, then pour into a sterilized bottle. Store.
PREP: 2 minutes   COOK: 6 minutes
MAKES: 15-ounce (500ml) bottle

Parsley oil

1¾ ounces (50g) parsley,
  including stems
1 green jalapeño chile

1¾ cups (400ml) extra-virgin
  olive oil

Fill a bowl with cold water and ice cubes. Bring a medium saucepan of water to a boil. Once boiling, add the parsley, stems and all, and blanch for 5 seconds. Add to the ice water. Squeeze any water out of the parsley, add to a blender with the jalapeño and olive oil, and blend until smooth. Pour the mixture through a cheesecloth-lined bowl, tie the top, and hang on a faucet or hook with the bowl underneath to catch the oil. Let drip out for 1 hour. Pour into a sterilized bottle and store. PREP: 1 hour 5 minutes
COOK: 5 minutes   MAKES: 14-ounce (400ml) bottle

Chopped herb oil

4 cornichons
1 tablespoon capers
1 bunch of mint, basil, parsley
zest and juice of ½ lemon

1 garlic clove, grated
1 tablespoon red wine vinegar
8 tablespoons olive oil
salt and ground black pepper

Coarsely chop the cornichons and capers, then add the herbs and
chop it all together. Scoop into a bowl, add the lemon zest and
juice, then add the garlic, vinegar, and olive oil. Taste and season
with salt and pepper. Serve. Best eaten the day it's made.
PREP: 5 minutes   COOK: 0 minutes
MAKES: a small bowl (5½ ounces/150g) enough for 2 to 3 people

Indian curry leaf & seed oil

8 tablespoons peanut oil
1 tablespoon black
    mustard seeds
1 teaspoon coriander seeds

½ teaspoon cumin seeds
15 curry leaves
1 dried Kashmiri red chile, torn
½ teaspoon flaky sea salt

Heat the oil in a small saucepan over medium heat. Once hot (you
can test by dropping a couple of mustard seeds in, and if they
sizzle it's ready), add the mustard seeds, coriander, and cumin
seeds and fry for 1 minute. Add the curry leaves and dried chile.
Once the leaves are crispy, remove from the heat and add to a
bowl. Season with flaky salt and serve.
PREP: 2 minutes   COOK: 4 minutes   MAKES: 7-ounce (200g) jar

Aioli is really addictive. You'll find yourself eating it with everything, but it's perfect with fish soup and roast chicken.

Garlic aioli

with lemon

PREP TIME: 2 minutes   COOK TIME: 0 minutes   MAKES: 1¾ cups (400ml)

• •

2 medium egg yolks
scant ½ cup (100ml) extra-virgin
   olive oil
1¼ cups (300ml) mild olive oil
juice of 1 lemon
1 garlic clove, grated
salt

Add the egg yolks to a medium bowl and whisk. Pour both oils into a measuring jug or cup and very slowly whisk the oil in, drop by drop. Once the aioli starts thickening, you can be a bit quicker with pouring in the oils.

Once all the oils have been added and it is a thick mayonnaise, add half the lemon juice and the garlic and mix well. Season with a good amount of salt, taste, and add any extra lemon juice, if needed.

• •

STORE/MAKE IT VEGAN
Store any leftovers in a sterilized jar in the refrigerator for up to two weeks.

• •

Index

Emily Ezekiel

• •

London born and bred, Emily currently works as a food author, art director, and food and prop stylist in the heart of Hackney, East London. She has worked in the food industry for over 15 years, and during this period she has gathered a wealth of experience across an impressive portfolio of food-related, creative projects and clients. She has worked alongside the most well-respected and best-loved names in the industry, including Jamie Oliver, Nigella Lawson, and Anna Jones.

Acknowledgments

• •

My long-standing work wife, incredible friend, and continuous creative partner Issy Croker, for being the best photographer there is. Without you this book would be just an idea, you make it all come to life. Thank you for always having my back and being by my side in our careers.

Joseph Denison Carey for being my right-hand man, for cooking and testing most of the recipes. You kept us all going with your energy and love.

To my editor Kathy for being so utterly brilliant with my words and for always helping me out when I'm in a pickle and supporting me through this process. Thank you for all your help always. The designer Alice, for laying this book out and making it all look so lovely. Thank you to all the interns who came and helped us with the piles of dishes, dashes to the stores, and general brilliance. Finally, thank you to the person reading this book. Without you I wouldn't get to do what I love each year. May you cook and always be happy.

Hardie Grant North America
2912 Telegraph Ave
Berkeley, CA 94705
hardiegrantusa.com

Text © 2024 by Emily Ezekiel
Photographs © 2024 by Issy Croker
Illustrations © 2024 by Alice Chadwick

Published in the United States by Hardie Grant North America, an imprint of Hardie Grant Publishing Pty Ltd. Library of Congress Cataloging-in-Publication Data is available upon request
ISBN: 9781958417614
eBook ISBN: 9781958417621

Acquiring editor: Catie Ziller
Photographer: Issy Croker
Photography assistant: Joseph Denison Carey
Designer & illustrator: Alice Chadwick
Copy editor: Kathy Steer

Printed in China
FIRST EDITION

FSC — MIX
Paper | Supporting responsible forestry
www.fsc.org FSC® C020056

Hardie Grant
PUBLISHING